# THE BOOK OF
# JEWELRY

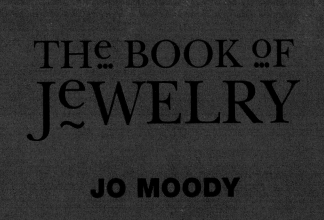

# THE BOOK OF JEWELRY

## JO MOODY

**CREATE YOUR OWN JEWELRY WITH BEADS,
CLAY, PAPIER-MÂCHÉ, FABRIC, AND OTHER
EVERYDAY ITEMS**

SIMON & SCHUSTER
New York  London  Toronto  Sydney  Tokyo  Singapore

SIMON & SCHUSTER

Rockefeller Center

1230 Avenue of the Americas

New York, New York 10020

Copyright © 1994 Quarto Inc.

This book was designed and produced by

Quarto Inc.

The Old Brewery, 6 Blundell Street

London N7 9BH, Great Britain

SENIOR EDITOR Jane Middleton
ART EDITOR Clare Baggaley
DESIGNER Debbie Mole
PICTURE RESEARCHER Laura Bangert
ILLUSTRATOR David Kemp
PHOTOGRAPHER Chas Wilder
PICTURE MANAGER Giulia Hetherington
ART DIRECTOR Moira Clinch
EDITORIAL DIRECTOR Sophie Collins

Typeset by Central Southern Typesetters, Eastbourne, UK
Manufactured by Eray Scan Pte. Ltd., Singapore
Printed by Star Standard Industries Pte. Ltd., Singapore

10  9  8  7  6  5  4  3  2  1

Library of Congress Catalogue Card Number:
Moody, Jo.
    The book of jewelry: create your own jewelry with beads, clay
papier-mâché, fabric and other everyday items / by Jo Moody.
        p.     cm.
    ISBN 0-671-89096-4
    1. Jewelry making.    I. Title.
TT212.M66    1994                                       94-1812
745.594'2—dc20                                          CIP

# 4
# CLaY & PLaSTIC

# 5
# TREaSURES FOR FRee

# Introduction

■ ■ ■ **The craft of jewelry making is no longer restricted to highly trained professionals working with precious metals and stones. Today's designs are an eclectic mix of tradition, fashion and fun, created out of the most basic materials, using simple techniques.**

The projects in this book are designed to inspire, and little time or skill is required to put them together. The basic components are relatively inexpensive and are readily available from the mall, specialist craft outlets, or mail order suppliers.

Bead jewelry is a good place to start, and once you have mastered the basic principles of attaching the findings, there will be no end to what you can make.

Buttons are not commonly associated with making jewelry, but with just a little imagination and wit they can be used to wonderful effect. Look twice before you decide to throw that blouse out, because its buttons could be the foundation for a necklace or bracelet!

Fabric is currently one of the most fashionable jewelry mediums, and talented designers are producing wonderfully

wearable accessories that sell for considerable amounts of money. Stunning fabric jewelry can be made using scraps, and only basic sewing skills are needed.

Paper is not a material that springs to mind for jewelry, but a quick glance at the projects in Chapter 4 reveals its versatility. It is surprisingly easy to create unusual and attractive pieces out of paper.

Clay is a medium that has recently become available in new and exciting forms. Synthetic polymer or air-drying clay such as Fimo and Das are easy to use and are much better suited to use in the home, as they do not need to be fired at high temperatures in special kilns. Less traditional than clay are the sheet plastics such as acrylic and plexiglass.

The last chapter in this book, Treasures for Free, shows you how to make something out of nothing. It is amazing how creative you can be with an old tin can or pebbles picked up on the beach!

We hope that you enjoy making the projects as much as we have enjoyed putting this book together, and that you will feel inspired to go on and experiment with different ideas to create your own individual designs. ■ ■ ■

*leather thong*  *thick wire*  *fine wire*  *nylon fishing line*

# Tools and materials

■ ■ ■ **The projects in this book are easy to make, and most of them can be put together at the kitchen table. Whichever room you do choose, it should be well lit without casting shadows, which make handling small, fiddly pieces very difficult. If you are using heavy-duty adhesives, the room should be well ventilated.**

A crafts board is also useful – the jeweler's equivalent of a cook's chopping board. Made from chipboard, particle board or similar, it protects the table from damage and provides a good surface for gluing, cutting, and painting.

Keep findings, beads, etc., organized and dust-free in a set of drawers such as the ones used to store nails and screws. Matchboxes and clean jars will work just as well.

Although you don't need much in the way of specialist tools, there are a few items that are worth investing in, as they will produce a more professional finish.

The first and most important is a good pair of small jewelry or watchmaker's pliers with fine, smooth tips. If you

*hand drill*  *jeweler's saw*  *tin snips*

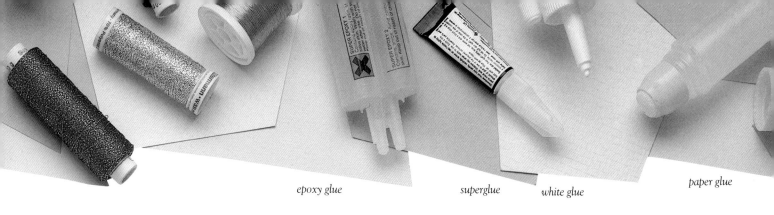

epoxy glue                superglue        white glue                    paper glue

can afford to, buy both round-nosed and needle-nosed pliers, preferably with cutters for trimming wire. Needle-nosed pliers are more versatile, so if you can only afford one pair, go for them. If your pliers do not have a cutting edge, you will need a pair of side cutters to shorten wires and head pins; a sturdy pair of household scissors will also do the job.

A few projects in this book involve the use of a basic power drill, the type found in most tool boxes. You could also invest in a precision crafts drill, which is smaller and easier to hold, giving greater control. You will also need a fine-bladed scroll saw or jeweler's saw to cut out shapes from sheet plastics like acrylic.

A wide variety of threads is available, and there are no set rules to govern which you should choose. It depends on your chosen design and the size and weight of your beads.

Silk and cotton both hang well, but they are not very hard-wearing and are therefore unsuitable for heavier beads. Leather thongs and laces are strong and hard-wearing, making them ideal for heavier beads and pendants. Nylon fishing line, fine enough to pass through the tiniest of beads, is strong, and invisible.  ■ ■ ■

small ball end hammer

scissors      craft knife

wire cutters      needle-nosed pliers      round-nosed pliers

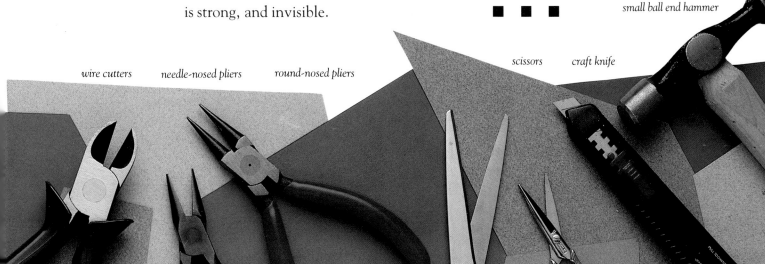

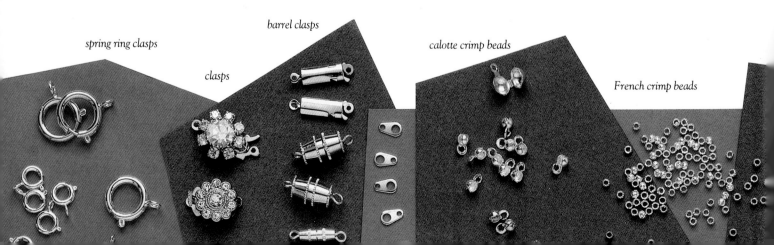

*earring backs*    *flat pad posts*    *ear wires*    *screw findings*    *flat pad clip*    *wire loops for earrings*

# *Findings* ■ ■ ■ **Almost all jewelry making involves the use of findings. These are the basic components that turn your designs into neatly finished necklaces, earrings, bracelets, and brooches. Once again, there are no hard and fast rules for their use; it is up to the designer to use them as creatively as possible to achieve the right look and get each piece to hang correctly.**

The most important findings are clasps, head pins, jump rings, ear fittings, and brooch backs. They are readily available in a choice of precious and non-precious metals and can be highly decorative. Clasps are formed of two pieces which are attached to each end of a necklace or bracelet. When joined together, they secure the piece at the neck or wrist. Clasps come in a variety of forms. Barrel clasps and spring rings are the simplest and most discreet in appearance. Snap clasps are far more elaborate: they can be gilt, silver-plated, or textured, and some are set with pearls and rhinestone. Head pins and eye pins are wire pins of varying lengths. A head pin has a flat head at one end, similar to a dressmaker's pin, and an eye pin has one preformed loop, or eye.

*spring ring clasps*    *barrel clasps*    *clasps*    *calotte crimp beads*    *French crimp beads*

*kidney wires*

*hoop earrings*

*eye pins*

*head pins*  *perforated ring base*

*end spacer bar*

*decorative end spacer*

They are primarily used for linking beads together and are especially useful when making earrings. Jump rings are circular metal rings that are not completely joined together. They are opened at the joint with pliers, used to link two or more pieces together, then closed again with pliers. They should always be opened sideways to keep them from breaking. Ear fittings come in all shapes and sizes to suit both pierced and unpierced ears. Many of them have loops which can be opened for attaching head pins, eye pins, or wires. Brooch backs also come in a variety of styles, and decoration can be either sewn or stuck in place depending on the design. Rondelles and tips are used to cover the collection of knots at the end of necklaces or earrings made from more than one strand of beads. Crimp beads are used to finish threaded bead jewelry, securing the ends and providing a loop for attaching the clasp. French crimp beads are the tiniest; they are used to finish pieces strung on nylon, silk, or fishing line. End spacer bars attach the strands of a necklace or bracelet to a clasp, they also keep the strands set apart, or spaced. They range from the simple to the ornate, and some of the fancier filigree spacer bars can be used as the base for earrings or pendants.                                  ■ ■ ■

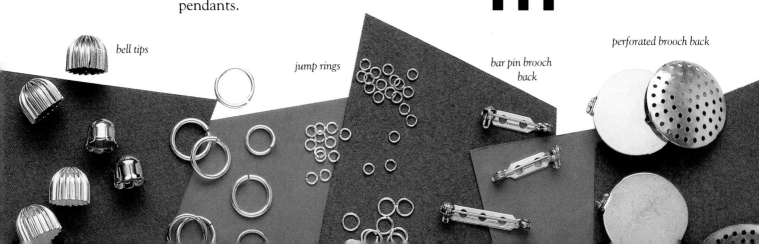

*bell tips*

*jump rings*

*bar pin brooch
back*

*perforated brooch back*

# Design ideas ■ ■ ■

It is often said that there is nothing new in the world, and it is true that many of the most unusual or innovative pieces of jewelry are inspired by familiar, everyday objects. Inspiration for designs can come from almost anywhere, though frequently inspiration comes simply from the materials at hand.

The past has always been a huge influence on jewelry designers, since not only the techniques but also many of the materials were first used thousands of years ago. The ancient Egyptian, Roman, and Celtic civilizations provide a rich source of inspiration, as do the more recent Arts and Crafts and Art Deco periods. A visit to a museum is a good occasion to look at jewelry or be inspired by the renditions of period jewelry in paintings. Libraries are an excellent source of illustrated books and old magazines, with plenty of original ideas to recreate in your own way.

Mother Nature produces one of the greatest design source libraries available, and it costs nothing. Flora and fauna, rock and minerals, insect and animal life can all prompt the imagination. The sky has provided us with sun,

moon, and star motifs, all perfect for interpreting into jewelry, and the sea washes shells up on the beach and sculpts pebbles into interesting shapes. It is a good idea to keep a plastic bag in your pocket, especially out walking, so that you can bring home things that inspire you.

Most jewelers use the materials they work with as their source of inspiration. Beads and fabrics can be thrown together haphazardly to create striking and unusual combinations, paints can be experimented with, and clay molded to unusual shapes, depending on the mood of the moment. Turn to ordinary household items – bits of string, spare buttons, or scraps of fabric – or simple kitchen equipment such as cookie cutters or cheesecloth. Many adventurous designers seek inspiration from unorthodox materials.

When you design your own jewelry, each piece will carry your individual stamp, as no two people interpret even the same design source the same way. One of the secrets of success is not to be afraid of experimenting with both the traditional and the unusual, and if you keep an open mind and a sense of humor, you will begin to see potential in almost anything around you. ■ ■ ■

# Quick and easy

Before you try your hand at any of the longer projects in the book, these two pages offer a few easy ideas for you to practice your skills. All use cheap, readily available materials and none require special skills.

**WRAPPED IN SILVER**
Pieces of slate can be wrapped in silver wire to make stylish and unusual pendants. The slate can be left natural or varnished to give a glossy sheen. The wire should be flattened slightly with a hammer, then wrapped around the slate, leaving a loop at the top for a chain.

**FESTIVE PLUM PUDDINGS** Add a touch of humor to the festive season with these plum-pudding earrings made from polymer clay, or adapt the idea to make your own designs – Christmas trees, Santa Claus, and even Christmas cakes would look just as good! Insert eye pins into the pudding before baking the clay according to the manufacturer's directions. If they are loose after baking, take out the eye pins, add a drop of strong glue and reinsert. Then simply add ear wires.

**BUTTON CHARM BRACELET** This is a great way of using up odd buttons found in the bottom of your sewing box. Simply use triangle bales or jump rings and pliers to attach the shank fittings of a selection of buttons onto nylon thread or a chain bracelet. Experiment with different fastenings, and add beads to the thread if desired. Here, self-cover buttons are used to link beaded lengths of thread.

## AUTUMN LEAVES

You can make earrings in minutes from polymer clay, using a fallen leaf as a template. Try experimenting with different leaf shapes or different-colored clay and paints. Roll a layer of Fimo about ¼ inch thick. Lay a leaf on top and roll again, then cut around the leaf template. Make a small Fimo loop at the top to hold the ear wire, and bake in the oven following the manufacturer's instructions.

## PERFECT PEBBLES

Next time you take a walk on a beach, keep a lookout for unusual small pebbles with holes worn in them by the sea. You can add shells, either choosing examples which already have holes or using a hand drill to make them. They can be strung on a leather thong to make a necklace. Knots keep each pebble and shell separate.

## ROMANY HOOPS

Brass curtain rings can be transformed into gypsy-style earrings with ease. Different-sized rings can be placed inside each other or linked together to create dramatic drops. Use short lengths of thick copper wire to link the rings together bending the loops with pliers.

## CLASSIC CRYSTAL

Faceted crystal reflects the light beautifully and always looks elegant and expensive. Ready-mounted stones need only to have earring backs glued in place; the drops are easy to make using triangle bales, first slipped through the loop of the ear clip, then tightened with pliers through the top of each drop.

## WITTY WIRE EARRINGS

Plastic-coated electrician's wire comes in a variety of bright colors and can be used to make simple drop earrings. You can vary the lengths of the loops or fan them out to create different finished effects. Glue loops made from folded 2-inch lengths of wire into one end of a pair of crimp beads, glue eye pins into the other end, and attach an ear wire to each earring.

# BEADS & BUTTONS

# 1
...

# BEaDS&
# BuTToNS
...    ...

# Beads and buttons

■ ■ ■ **The astonishing variety of fake jewels, buttons, and beads widely available from stores or by mail order is a jewelry designer's idea of heaven. Simply string them together, or loop and weave them into more intricate designs. The possibilities are limitless, and the basic techniques are some of the easiest to be found in jewelry making.**

Beads can be fashioned from almost anything, and they come in a wonderful kaleidoscopic range of colors. They have been used to make jewelry since the beginning of civilization. Many ancient techniques are still employed today, and designs such as millefiori (see page 32) are as popular now as they were when they first appeared in Venice in the 14th century.

Another design currently enjoying favor dates from the 19th century, when trade links were built up between the western world and the African continent. The Venetians, together with the Russians, Dutch, and notably the Bohemians produced beads of such quality that they were highly coveted by the Africans. These colorful and boldly patterned beads were accepted as payment for gold, ivory, and, sadly, slaves and are known as African Trade Beads. Original beads can still be found, and they are extremely collectible.

Old and antique buttons make great bracelets and earrings, and with a little ingenuity, they can be joined together to create dramatic necklaces and pendants. Look for them at tailgate sales or on old clothes at yard sales, and use any odd ones at the bottom of your button box. ■ ■ ■

# Basic techniques for making bead jewelry

Making your own jewelry is easy once you have mastered the basic techniques. The simple projects on these pages illustrate the rudiments of jewelry construction step by step and show how to work with the most frequently used findings.

## Cabochon Earrings

*These elegant earrings are a perfect example of how easy it is to make your own jewelry. The beads are simply threaded onto a* *head pin and then joined to an ear clip with a jump ring. Special flat-backed beads known as cabochons are a stylish way of concealing the ear clips.*

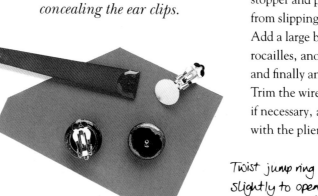

**2** Thread a small rocaille onto each head pin to act as a stopper and prevent the pin from slipping straight through. Add a large bead, a few more rocailles, another large bead, and finally another rocaille. Trim the wire with wire cutters if necessary, and turn a loop with the pliers.

*Twist jump ring slightly to open*

### Materials
. . .
2 ear clips with integral loops
·
2 flat-backed cabochons
·
Epoxy glue
·
2 head pins
·
Small rocaille beads
·
4 large beads
·
Wire cutters (optional)
·
Pliers
·
Jump rings
. . .

**1** Glue an ear clip to the back of each cabochon so that the loop protrudes just below the bead. Leave until completely dry.

**3** Open a jump ring with the pliers and insert it through both the loop at the top of the head pin and the loop on the ear clip. Close carefully, making sure the two ends meet.

# Simple Stringing

*Before making your necklace, you need to decide how long you want it to be – a standard necklace is between 18 and 20 inches and a choker is from 14 to 16 inches. Next you need to select a suitable thread. There are a number of different types available, the choice depends on the weight of the beads and the size of the hole. Silk, cotton, and nylon are all strong and flexible.*

## Materials
• • •
Strong cotton thread
•
2 eye or head pins (or silver wire)
•
Superglue
•
2 bell tips
•
Wire cutters
•
Pliers
•
Selection of beads
•
Rhinestone rondelles
•
Needle
•
Necklace clasp
•
Jump rings
• • •

1 Cut five or six strands of thread to the desired length plus a little extra for knotting the ends. Knot the threads securely through the loop (eye) at one end of an eye pin. If you don't have an eye pin, snip the flat end off a head pin with wire cutters and use pliers to turn it into a loop. Or cut off a short length of silver wire, turn a loop in one end, then knot the threads through the loop as before. Adding a dot of glue to the knot helps to strengthen it.

*Eye pin inserted through bell tip*

2 To create a neat finish, the pin is inserted through the hole at the top of a bell tip. Trim the pin with wire cutters and then turn another loop using pliers. This second loop is used to attach a necklace clasp (see Step 4).

3 Having worked out your design, string the beads onto the threads, adding the rhinestone rondelle spacers to give a little sparkle. Tiny beads or disks can also be used as spacers between beads to create interesting effects. The necklace doesn't necessarily need a central focal bead, but it is essential that the two sides are identical.

4 This shows in detail how the necklace clasp is attached. Knot the ends of the thread to an eye or head pin as in Step 1, and push through the bell tip as in Step 2. Undo the necklace clasp. Using pliers, open up a jump ring by twisting it sideways. Insert the ring through the loop on one side of the clasp, then through a bell tip, and then close it up with pliers. Repeat for the second part of the necklace clasp.

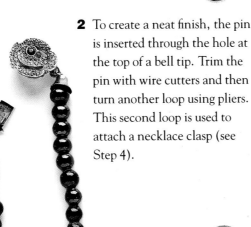

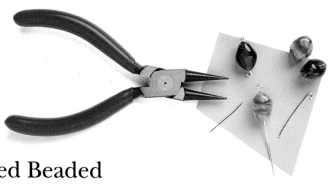

# Linked Beaded Necklace

*Stringing beads onto thread is not the only way of creating necklaces; they can also be linked together using eye and head pins. This method is frequently used to make earrings, too, and it is very easy to achieve spectacular results. The clever addition of chain links between the beads on this necklace creates a sophisticated finished piece.*

**1** If using head pins, the flat "head" will need to be snipped off with wire cutters and a loop turned at one end with pliers. Insert a pin through one large bead, trim the wire, and turn a loop at the end. Push a pin through another bead, open the loop slightly, and link it to the loop on the previous bead. Continue linking the beads together in this way in groups of two or three.

Open loop

**3** Use pliers to open up the loop on one part of the necklace clasp. Push this through the last link in the chain on one side. Close the loop carefully, making sure the two ends are as close together as possible. Repeat for the other side of the necklace.

## Materials

• • •

Eye pins or head pins

•

Wire cutters

•

Pliers

•

Selection of beads

•

Length of chain with wide links

•

Jump rings

•

Necklace clasp

• • •

**2** To attach the chain, first decide how many links are required. Using pliers, open the link one beyond the length required by snipping the join. It is much easier to join a fully closed chain link to an opened loop on the bead than to try and close up an open link. Push the open loop through the chain and close to secure. Continue working in the same way until you have a necklace of the desired length.

# Pierced Beaded Brooch

*The perforated or pierced brooch finding used here comes in two parts: a pierced front section with claws, which can be embroidered with beads, and a back plate with a brooch fastening, which is secured over the front part by folding the claws over it with pliers. Similar clip ear fittings are also available (see Romantic Lace Rosettes, page 46).*

Sew in and out of holes

**1** Thread a needle, then knot the thread to one side of the perforations. Thread on the beads to create a string the desired length. Take the needle and thread back through the holes and secure on the wrong side, creating a bead loop. Repeat for the other side, varying the beads used. "Sew" smaller beads to the top by weaving the thread through the holes, then the bead, and back through the holes and up again for the next bead.

**2** Add a single long string of beads to the center front point and continue to build up your design, "sewing" the beads in the required position.

## Materials
∙ ∙ ∙
Perforated brooch finding
∙
Thread
∙
Needle
∙
Selection of brightly colored beads
∙
Superglue
∙
Pliers
∙ ∙ ∙

**3** Dab a dot of glue on each point where the thread is secured or knotted. Place the back plate over the threads on the wrong side of the perforations and use pliers to fold over the claws that keep it in place.

# Dividing Strands

*A more intricate finishing can be achieved by dividing the strands and working on each individually before bringing them back together through one bead. The loops created can be as long as you like to suit your design, and you can work on more than two strands if you prefer.*

Calotte

**1** Cut two pieces of nylon thread to the desired length plus a little extra to allow for the loops and knotting. Knot the threads together at one end and, using pliers, crimp a calotte over the knot. To do this, separate the two sides of the calotte, slip it over the knot, and shape the ends back together with pliers.

**2** Begin by treating the threads as one and string on beads in the required pattern. Divide the strands, then work on each individually, threading beads onto both strands.

**3** When you have completed the loop, bring the strands back together again, threading them both through one bead. Continue dividing and bringing the strands back together again until you reach the length required, remembering to keep both sides of the necklace exactly the same.

Loop on screw clasp

**4** Knot the ends together close to the beads and crimp a calotte over the knot as before. Open the loops on the screw clasp with pliers and insert them through the loops of each calotte to secure.

**Materials**

Nylon thread

Pliers

Calotte crimp bead

Screw necklace clasp

Selection of large and small beads

Rhinestone rondelles

# Knotting

*Necklaces can be strung on colored threads to coordinate with the beads or textured threads to create interest. A sophisticated and professional look can be achieved by knotting the thread between each bead, which has the added advantage of stopping the beads from spilling everywhere if the necklace breaks. The knot must be large enough not to slip through the bead, so use either thick or several strands of fine thread.*

### Materials
• • •
Strong thread to coordinate with the beads
•
Selection of beads
•
Needle
•
Calottes
•
Pliers
•
Jump rings
•
Necklace clasp
• • •

**1** Cut several strands of thread to the desired length plus at least half as much again to allow for the knots. Make a practice knot to check that it won't slip through the bead. Add more strands of thread if necessary for a thicker knot. String on a bead and make a loose knot, taking the thread through the loop of the knot twice.

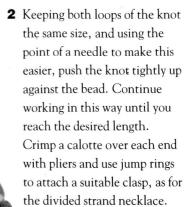

**2** Keeping both loops of the knot the same size, and using the point of a needle to make this easier, push the knot tightly up against the bead. Continue working in this way until you reach the desired length. Crimp a calotte over each end with pliers and use jump rings to attach a suitable clasp, as for the divided strand necklace.

This pretty pastel and pearl necklace is threaded onto several strands

# *Tiffany-style necklace*

of silk which
are divided and

brought back together again,

creating a beautiful delicate

effect. The large beads are

styrofoam

balls that have

been given an

expensive-looking marbled finish by

clever painting with nail polish and

watercolors.

**1** Pierce a hole through the
center of each styrofoam ball
with a knitting needle or
wooden skewer to form a bead.

### Materials
• • •
Medium and large
styrofoam balls
•
Knitting needle or
wooden skewer
•
Nail polish in a
variety of colors
•
Watercolor paints
•
Metallic felt-tip pen
•
Silk thread
•
Beeswax cake
•
Selection of small
beads and bugles
in differing sizes
•
Fine needle
•
Superglue
• • •

**2** Using a stippling motion,
decorate the styrofoam balls
with nail polish and watercolor
paint to create a marbled effect.
Leave each coat to dry before
applying the next. The
watercolor paint sits on top of
the nail polish, adding to the
effect. You may find it easier to
paint the balls while they are
on the needle or skewer.

**3** Complete the paint effect on
the beads with lines drawn in
metallic felt-tip pen.

Divide strands

Bring strands
back together

**4** Decide on the length of the finished necklace, including the tassel. Cut the silk thread into four equal strands, each the required length. Pull the strands through the beeswax cake to coat them; this makes them stronger and easier to separate. Place them all together and fold in half to find the center back. The necklace is worked from this point to the center front, treating each side the same to create a symmetrical design.

**5** Thread all four strands through some small beads and bugles to sit along the center back neck to start the necklace. Next divide into two 2-strand sections. Work each of these identically, then bring them back together by threading all four strands through one bead. Continue threading beads until you reach the center front.

**6** Take all eight threads (both sides) through two small beads, then through a medium styro – foam bead, followed by a couple of smaller beads. Divide in half again and take each set of four strands through a few small beads, a styrofoam bead, and a few more beads. Bring all eight back together through the final large styrofoam bead.

Take needle back
through bugles

**7** Each strand is now worked individually to create the tassel. Thread bugle beads onto each strand and finish with a small pearl. Wrap the strand back over the pearl, and using a needle, thread the strand back through the bugle beads. Knot each strand securely to itself at a convenient point and anchor the knot with a dot of glue.

Weaving beads on a loom is a traditional craft, used for centuries to make all kinds of jewelry. This bracelet is worked in pearly-

# *Art deco beadwork*

white, black, and silver-gray, in a simple design that is evocative of the 1920s. It is a perfect introduction to the basic techniques and will inspire you to create your own designs. The earrings are worked in the same colors to coordinate, but are woven by hand rather than on the loom.

Put knot over this end

Put loops over this end

Warp threads

**1** Measure your wrist loosely with a tape measure. If the weaving area of your loom is longer than this, measure the loom from end to end, between the places where the thread is fastened. Add 5 inches to your wrist or

## Materials
▪ ▪ ▪
Beadweaving loom
▪
Pearly-white, black and silver-gray beads
▪
Tape measure
▪
Fine strong white thread
▪
Fine beading needle
▪ ▪ ▪

loom measurement (whichever is bigger), then double this and cut six threads to this length. Fold them in half and knot the loose ends together so that you have a loop of threads at one end.

**2** Put the loops over one of the pegs on the loom and the knot over the other end. Turn the bar until the threads are almost taut, then separate the threads and spread them out over the dividers. (Don't worry if the threads are farther apart than your beads are wide, as you can tighten as you go.) Tighten the fitting to make the threads as taut as possible. These are the warp threads.

**3** Take a long thread in your beading needle and thread on 11 white beads. Place the thread with the beads on the warp threads about 1 inch from the looped end, and tuck each bead into the spaces between the threads. Leaving a long end for weaving in later, push the beads down so that they jut out underneath the warp threads and then bring the needle back through the beads, keeping them under the warp. Hold the end of the thread so that it doesn't come straight through, and pull the row tight.

Eye of bracelet fastening

Bar

**7** To make the bar of the fastening, go back to the start of the weaving and pick up nine beads as in Step 5. Pick up seven beads for the next row and five for the following row and work as before. Add three rows of three beads, then thread on 15 beads and take the needle back through the last row to make a loop of beads. Flatten the loop so that you have two rows of nine beads, including the three beads of the last row. Join these two rows together by stitching into the first bead on one row followed by the second on the other, the third on the first row, etc. Finish by weaving the thread back through a few rows to fasten off.

**8** Take the remaining ends of threads back through a few rows and cut close to the weaving. Remove the bracelet from the loom and thread all the ends of the warp threads back into the bracelet in the same manner.

**5** To make the "eye," pick up nine beads and lay them centrally on the warp threads. Bring the needle back through the beads as before, passing the needle through the gap instead of around the end. Pick up seven beads for the next row and work as before. Work three rows of two beads at one side of the seven, then repeat the other side to match.

**6** Slide seven beads on the thread and lay them over the top of the rows of two beads. Take the needle through the first two beads underneath the warp threads, then take it over the warp for the next three so that it is not caught in, going back under for the last two beads. Repeat this row, then join these last two rows together by sewing into the first bead on one row, then the second on the other, the third bead on the first row, etc. Weave the thread back through a few rows to fasten off.

**4** Working from the chart, pick up the beads as shown for each row and add them to the warp threads in the same way as for Step 3. When nearing the end of a thread, leave a long tail after finishing a row, and start another thread by running the needle through the last few rows. If you reach the end of the loom before you have worked the required length, turn the bar at the end to move the weaving on. Continue weaving until your bracelet is about 1 inch shorter than your wrist measurement.

# Thousand-flower necklace

Millefiori or "thousand flower" beads were originally made from glass by the Venetians and were highly prized around the world. Today, the same principles used in the 14th century can be applied to polymer clay to create exquisite beads. Different-colored clays are rolled together to create the "millefiori cane"; this is then sliced and the slices used to cover a base bead. The technique is much easier to master than it appears.

**1** Roll out two sheets of different-colored clay with a rolling pin, until they are approximately ⅛ inch thick. Place one sheet on top of the other and roll them together like a jelly roll to create a spiral effect.

## Materials

Fimo or similar polymer clay, in 5 or 6 different colors

Rolling pin

Craft knife

Knitting needle

Eye pins

Selection of small metal beads or washers

Pliers

Ear wires

Thread

Necklace clasp

**2** Take another color and, using the palms of your hands, roll into a long log shape 1 inch in diameter. Use a rolling pin to roll out another sheet in a contrasting color to ⅛ in thick, then wrap it around the log. Smooth the seam with the rolling pin, then continue rolling it out to create a longer, thinner piece. Cut this into five equal lengths.

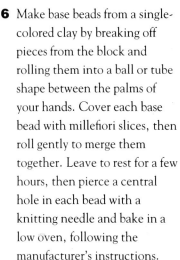

**3** Roll out another log in a different color as for Step 2, but make it slightly narrower and omit the wrapping. Cut it into five equal lengths. Assemble the millefiori cane with the spiral in the center and the five wrapped logs alternating with the smaller, single-color logs as shown. Gently press together.

**4** Wrap the cane in another contrasting sheet of clay (or repeat one of the colors used for the spiral) and roll gently and evenly until the diameter is about ¼ inch.

**6** Make base beads from a single-colored clay by breaking off pieces from the block and rolling them into a ball or tube shape between the palms of your hands. Cover each base bead with millefiori slices, then roll gently to merge them together. Leave to rest for a few hours, then pierce a central hole in each bead with a knitting needle and bake in a low oven, following the manufacturer's instructions.

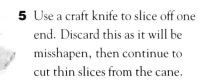

**5** Use a craft knife to slice off one end. Discard this as it will be misshapen, then continue to cut thin slices from the cane.

**7** To make the earrings, thread the beads onto an eye pin (eye at the top) with small metal beads or washers between each bead. Turn the bottom of the pin under with pliers to secure the beads, then attach an ear wire to the eye of the pin. Thread the remaining beads to make a necklace, finishing with a necklace clasp.

These simple eye-catching beads are made using the styrofoam balls found in craft stores. They provide an ideal base for many pieces of jewelry and can be painted and decorated in a variety of ways.

# Elegant black and white beads

## Materials

- Large, medium and small styrofoam balls
- Craft knife
- Ear clips with integral loops
- Double epoxy glue
- Newspaper
- Wallpaper paste
- White acrylic paint
- Paint brush
- Wooden skewers
- Technical drawing pen (or nib and waterproof ink)
- Varnish
- Selection of small beads
- Eye and head pins
- Pliers
- Jump rings
- Strong thread
- Needle
- Necklace clasp

**1** Cut one large styrofoam ball in half with a sharp craft knife. Glue an ear clip to each flat side using double epoxy. Leave to dry.

**3** When the papier-mâché is completely dry, paint with two coats of white acrylic paint.

**2** Make up a quantity of wallpaper paste according to manufacturer's instructions. Tear newspaper into small, neat strips and cover each styrofoam ball piece with three or four layers of pasted paper, making sure the back of each ear clip is well covered. The papier-mâché means that the cut ball has a smooth finish and the ear clip is secure.

Leave balls on skewers until completely dry

**7** To make the necklace, follow the same process, omitting steps 1 and 2. To make the barrel-shaped beads, cut off the sides of a large styrofoam ball before covering with papier-mâché. Join enough beads together on strong thread to make the necklace the length required and finish by attaching a necklace clasp.

Eye pin

Small bead

**4** Take the remaining styrofoam balls and pierce the center of each with wooden skewers, gently twisting and pushing them through. Leave on the skewers and paint with two coats of acrylic paint. Stand in a suitable container or in modeling clay to dry.

Decorate earrings in the same way

**6** To assemble the earrings, thread a small bead and then the bottom styrofoam ball and another small bead onto a head pin. The small bead acts as a stopper and prevents the head pin from ripping through the styrofoam. Thread the middle bead onto an eye pin in the same way. Using pliers, turn the top of the head pin and loop through the eye of the next bead to secure. Attach a jump ring through the loop of the ear clip, turn the end of the eye pin, and join to the jump ring.

**5** Leaving the beads on the skewers, draw on a pattern using a technical drawing pen or a nib and waterproof ink. If you prefer, you can draw the design first in soft pencil, then rub it off with an eraser once the ink is dry. Cover each bead with three or four coats of varnish and leave to dry.

Top fashion designers frequently use beautiful buttons to perfect their expensive creations, and their ideas have trickled through to haberdashery departments,

# Button treasures

where you can now find a remarkable selection of buttons in every imaginable shape and color.

## Mother-of-Pearl Bracelet and Choker

*Nothing could be easier to make than this bracelet and choker set. Delicately shaded buttons are strung on a leather thong, creating a simple but effective contrast of textures.*

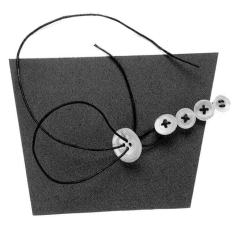

### Materials
. . .
Fine leather thong
•
Selection of
mother-of-pearl
buttons with four-
hole centers
•
Black cotton
thread
•
Needle
. . .

**1** Measure your wrist loosely and cut a length of leather thong twice this measurement plus about 2 inches to allow for the knot and loop. Fold the thong in half and thread each end through two holes of each button as shown, leaving a loop at the folded end the length of a button. Continue threading until the bracelet is a comfortable fit when the last button is fastened through the end loop. Knot the thong tightly at the back of the last button.

**2** Measure your neck and cut a piece of thong twice this length plus about 2 inches to allow for the fastening. Beginning and ending with a few small buttons, thread both ends of the thong through each button, crossing them over each other at the front as shown.

**3** The choker is fastened by inserting the last button at the looped end through a "buttonhole." Cut the thongs, leaving enough for two buttons plus ⅔ inch for binding. To create the buttonholes, leave space for one button, then bind the two pieces of thong tightly

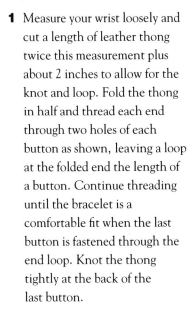

together by wrapping a length of double cotton thread over and over an area of approximately ⅓ inch.

**4** Thread the ends of the thread through a needle and push it through the binding to secure, dabbing on a dot of glue to strengthen. Allowing space for another button, repeat the binding at the very ends of the thong, securing it in the same way as before.

## Gilt Bracelet and Earrings

*Many buttons are almost too good to use in the conventional way, and a little lateral thinking turns them into splendid pieces of jewelry.*

### Materials
• • •

Selection of large gilt buttons with shanks

•

10 small gilt buttons with shanks

•

Tape measure

•

Strong thread

•

Jump rings

•

Needle

•

Small gilt beads

•

Bolt ring

•

Epoxy glue

•

Pliers

•

Earring posts and butterfly fastenings

• • •

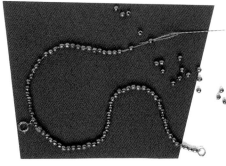

**1** Measure your wrist loosely and cut a length of thread twice this measurement plus 6 inches. Knot the thread to a jump ring and, using a needle, string on small gilt beads, attaching the bolt ring at the middle point. Continue to add beads until you have a length that fits your wrist when folded in half. Knot the end to the jump ring and take about 2 inches back through the beads. Dab glue on each knot to strengthen.

**2** Join the large gilt buttons to the bead bracelet by looping a jump ring through the shank of a button and around one of the bead threads. Close with pliers. Loop another jump ring through

the same shank and around the other bead thread. Join the other buttons in the same way, positioning them evenly along the beads.

**3** For each earring, link five small gilt buttons together, using pliers and jump rings as shown.

**4** Take two large gilt buttons and glue an ear post just above the shank on each one. Leave until completely dry. Link both ends of a button "chain" to the shank of each earring to form the drop.

# *Button tassel collar*

Pearl and gilt buttons and rich fabrics combine to striking effect in this gold and red collar.

**1** Cut out a rectangle measuring 4 × 20 inches from the main fabric, following the bias of the weave. Overcast the edge to prevent fraying.

**2** Fold second fabric in half, right sides together. Trace triangle template shown on this page on typing paper, then pin to fabric and cut out. Repeat six times so that you have seven sets of triangles.

template

**3** With right sides together, pin the two pieces of each triangle together. Sew the two short sides ⅜ inch from the edge, leaving the longest side unsewn. Trim the right-angled corner to ⅛ inch from stitching.

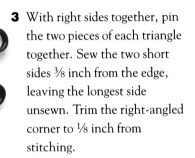

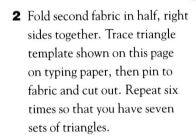

**4** Turn each triangle right side out and press, pushing the point out fully. Make a buttonhole vertically in each triangle. Each buttonhole should match the size of the button you have chosen, and the bottom point of the buttonholes should be ½ inch from the point of the triangle. Pink or whip the raw long edge of the triangle.

**5** Take the main fabric rectangle and, with the right side up, position the triangles on it. Position the first triangle so that one of its points aligns with the corner of the fabric and its base aligns with the long edge. Position, pin, and baste all the triangles, overlapping them by ½ inch. Now check the fit around your neck. The triangles can be moved apart or closer together, leaving a tail at one end of the collar. When the triangles are in the correct position, machine stitch them in place.

## Materials

• • •

¼ yard main fabric and thread to match

•

¼ yard second fabric and thread to match

•

Approx 10 buttons with shanks

•

Approx 100 other, mainly flat, buttons

•

Gold thread

•

Velcro fasteners or snaps

• • •

**6** Turn under both long sides of the main rectangle by ½ inch and baste. Fold the rectangle in half lengthwise so that the raw edges are concealed, and hemstitch the edges together on the wrong side of the collar, to within ½ inch of the ends. Remove the basting thread, fold in the raw edges at the ends of the fabric tube, and overcast neatly.

**7** To make a button tassel, thread a button onto a 15-inch length of gold thread. Take the ends of the thread, and pull the first button to the center of the length. Thread a needle onto each end and then "feed" your buttons onto both threads. When your tassel is the desired length, between 3 and 4 inches, knot the threads. Buttons with shanks look best used at the top or the bottom of the tassel. Leave the top ½ inch clear of buttons so that the fabric triangle will lie flat, then add the last button, knot, and cut thread.

**8** Button the tassels onto the collar. Here, the longest one is in the middle front, and the others are symmetrically shorter except for single longer strand at center back, but you can vary this according to taste.

**9** Sew the fastening onto the end of the collar. Velcro fasteners, snaps, or another button and buttonhole all work well.

### ∎∎∎
# INSPIRATIONS

**Beads and buttons can be simply strung or woven into intricate designs to make exquisite jewelry.**

**1** Beads and feathers are strung on wire to make a striking necklace and bracelet. *Anne Catherine Bull*

**2** Buttons are caught in tiny "pockets" sewn on net for this cowl. *Susie Freeman*

**3** Tiny glass rocaille beads are threaded in a Gothic-inspired design. *Debbie Siniska*

**4** Handmade papier-mâché beads linked with metal spirals create a strong modern look. *Deirdre Hawken*

**5** Beads made from modeling clay are given a bold hand-painted finish. *Pat Thomas*

**6** Fake pearls are strung together to create this elaborate multistrand necklace. *Jo Moody*

**7** Baroque and traditional pearls look good mixed with bright glass beads. *Jo Moody*

BEaDS&
BUTTONS

# FaBRIC & EMBRoIDERY

. . .

**ROMANTIC LACE ROSETTES**

. . .

**HIGH-TECH BROOCH AND EARRINGS**

. . .

**VIVID FELT BROOCH**

. . .

**VIBRANT KNITTED NECKLACE**

. . .

**SUMPTUOUS SILK JEWELRY**

. . .

**RICHNESS FROM RAGS**

# 2
...

# FᵃBRIC &
# EMBR...OIDERY

# Fabric and embroidery

■ ■ ■ **The use of fabric and embroidery in jewelry design has recently added a new dimension to the craft, and provides fresh challenges. Nothing is impossible when creating "soft" jewelry; you can let your imagination run riot.**

Anyone who knows how to use a needle can transform fabric remnants, scraps of embroidery thread, and leftover beads into stylish brooches, earrings, and even necklaces. Traditional techniques such as quilting and appliqué, beadwork, and collage can be applied to almost any type of fabric to great effect, producing wonderfully innovative jewelry. Machine embroidery is enjoying a big revival, thanks to talented young designers who are using it in new ways to create ornaments that deserve to be called works of art.

Inspired use of traditional tapestry and needle-point techniques can also produce good results. If you back your pieces with craft-weight interfacing and coordinating fabric, you can make unusual earrings or pendants. Trim them with beads and tassels to give them a sophisticated look for evening wear.

Don't be afraid to experiment, especially with unorthodox materials such as rubber and vinyl. Yarn, raffia, and string can be braided, woven, or knitted to create unusual jewelry, or dressed up with buttons and beads, sequins, or jewel stones for a more dramatic effect. Fabrics can be stiffened with a solution of white glue and molded into interesting shapes. The wonderful variety of fabric paints available allows you to design your own unique textiles.

If you give up thoughts of trying to recreate traditional jewelry, and are bold and adventurous with your use of colors and materials, the end results will be positive masterpieces! ■ ■ ■

# *Romantic lace rosettes* Perfect for a

bride, these pretty rosettes are simplicity itself to make. Use lace

trimmed with pearls for the big day, or choose any fabric and trim

to suit your outfit or mood: dramatic black lace or

velvet ribbon and crystal for evenings, or a

dotted or striped

grosgrain ribbon for

a sporty look.

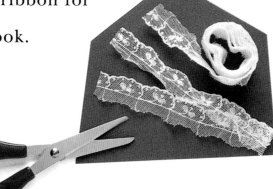

Raw edge

**1** Cut two 6¾-inch and two
8⅝-inch lengths of lace for the
earrings. Join the short ends of
each piece, making tiny French
seams to enclose the raw edges.

**3** Pull up the gathers carefully,
as tightly as possible without
breaking the thread, and
secure. Ease the gathers around
the center to form a rosette,
keeping the raw (straight) edge
of the lace to the wrong side.

## Materials
• • •
31½ inches of
¾-inch wide
cream edging
lace, preferably
with one scalloped
edge, plus a length
of wider lace with a
scalloped edge for
the brooch
•
Needle and thread
•
Perforated ear
fittings
•
Pearl beads
•
Pliers
•
Perforated brooch
back
• • •

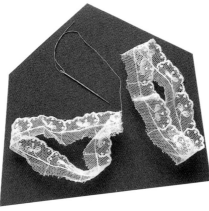

**2** Run a gathering thread along
the center of one 6¾-inch
length of lace.

Two pieces form double rosette

**4** Run a gathering thread along the center of one of the longer pieces. Place the rosette in the center and pull the gathers up around it. Fasten off and stitch the two together. Repeat, using the remaining pieces, for the second earring.

Single rosette brooch

**6** The brooch can be made as a single or double rosette in the same way, but with wider lace edging and a brooch fastening.

**5** Sew a pearl bead to the center of each double rosette, then stitch each rosette to a sieve ear fitting. Using pliers, bend the clips on the finding over the earring back to secure in place.

# High-tech brooch and earrings

Rubber is not a material that instantly comes to mind for making jewelry, but this colorful set shows what can be achieved if you set aside traditional influences. The matte black of the ribbed rubber floor covering is set off by brilliantly colored plastic disks and plastic drinking straws to create interesting and witty pieces.

## Materials

• • •

Piece of rubber floor covering at least 3½ × 4 inches

Scissors

Sturdy hole punch

Rubber tube

6 plastic disks

Power drill

Large jump rings

Pliers

Emery paper

Selection of brightly colored plastic drinking straws

Epoxy glue

Ear clips with integral loop

Brooch back

• • •

**1** Cut two 2-inch squares out of the rubber for the earrings and one 1½ in x 3½-inch piece for the brooch. Setting the brooch piece to one side for the moment, begin to make the earrings. Turn each square around to form a diamond then, using the hole punch, make three holes as shown – two at the side points and one at the top. Carefully cut off the top point above the hole.

**2** Cut two short lengths from the rubber tube and push them though the side holes of each diamond shape, pulling the points together. Trim the tube so that about ⅜ inch extends beyond the holes on each side.

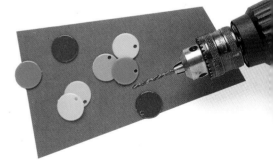

**3** Take six plastic disks and drill a hole close to the edge of each one with a power drill.

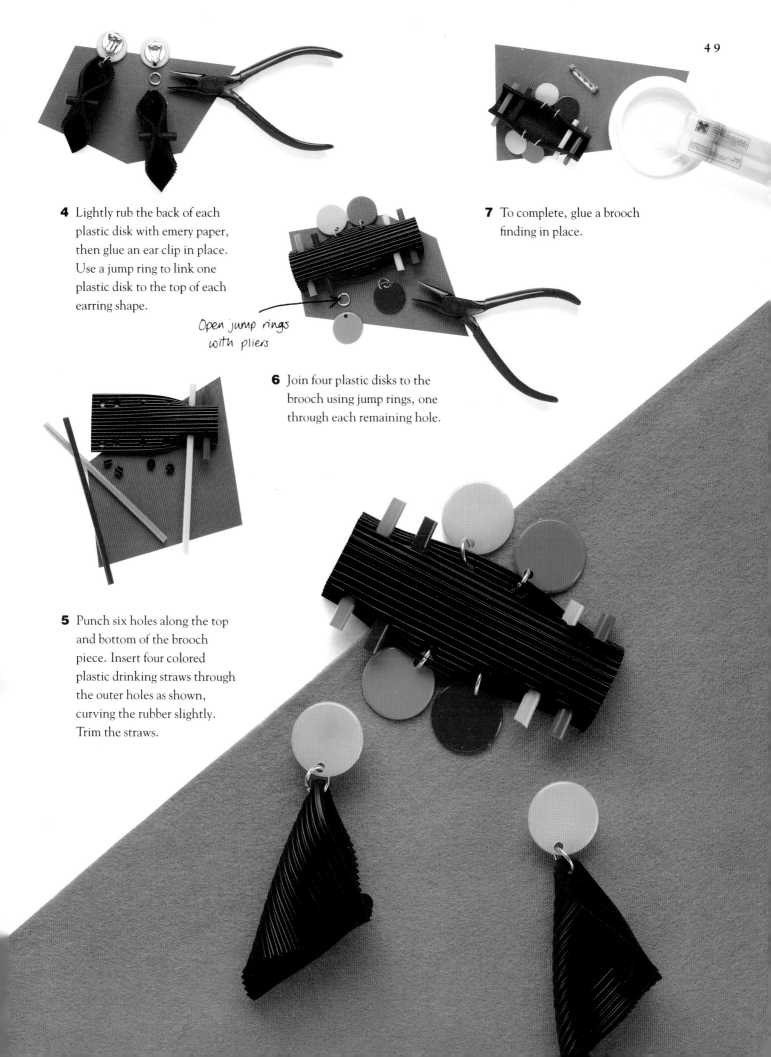

**4** Lightly rub the back of each plastic disk with emery paper, then glue an ear clip in place. Use a jump ring to link one plastic disk to the top of each earring shape.

*Open jump rings with pliers*

**5** Punch six holes along the top and bottom of the brooch piece. Insert four colored plastic drinking straws through the outer holes as shown, curving the rubber slightly. Trim the straws.

**6** Join four plastic disks to the brooch using jump rings, one through each remaining hole.

**7** To complete, glue a brooch finding in place.

This simple but effective design is made from scraps of felt sandwiched around craftweight interfacing to keep it rigid, and

## *Vivid felt brooch*

decorated with rocailles, bugle beads, and metallic thread. Here, it has been embellished with a silky golden tassel which is easily attainable and could be used to decorate many of the other pieces in the book. Vary the fabric with bright, clashing colors or a pretty print to produce different effects.

### Materials
• • •
Small pieces of felt in 2 colors
•
Scissors
•
Small piece of craft-weight interfacing
•
Pinking shears
•
Selection of rocailles and bugle beads
•
Metallic embroidery thread
•
Needle
•
Tassel
•
Craft glue suitable for jewelry and fabric that dries clear
•
Brooch finding
• • •

**1** Cut two 2-inch squares and one 1-inch square from felt in the main color. From the contrasting color cut one 1⅜-inch square and a small circle. Cut a 1¾-inch square from craftweight interfacing. Pink the edges of the smaller squares with pinking shears. Center the pieces on top of each other in this order – interfacing, 1 large square, contrast square, smaller square in main color and, finally circle (the remaining large square is not used until the end).

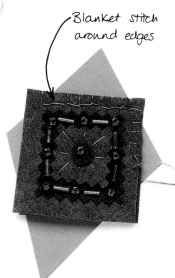

Blanket stitch around edges

**2** Place a rocaille in the center of the circle and sew in place, through all the layers, using metallic thread. With double thread, embroider eight straight stitches radiating out from the center as shown.

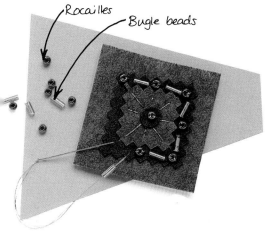

Rocailles   Bugle beads

**3** Still using double thread, stitch some rocailles and bugle beads all around the edges of the contrast square.

**4** Place the work on top of the remaining felt square, enclosing the interfacing, then join the two together using blanket stitch worked in double metallic thread.

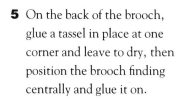

**5** On the back of the brooch, glue a tassel in place at one corner and leave to dry, then position the brooch finding centrally and glue it on.

# *Vibrant knitted necklace*

This ingenious knitted necklace was inspired by the brightly colored jewelry worn by African women. Different types of yarn can be used to create different effects: the necklace shown here uses a silky knitting ribbon, but you could experiment with anything from a velvety chenille to a textured bouclé yarn.

**1** Using Size 13 (9 mm) needles, cast on 12 stitches and work in stocking stitch (knit 1 row, purl 1 row) until you have reached the desired length for your necklace. (You can use smaller needles and alter the number of stitches to create a different effect.) Bind off, then sew up the side seam to form a tube.

### Materials
• • •
Ribbon knitting yarn
•
Size 13 (9 mm) knitting needles
•
Styrofoam balls
•
Acrylic paints
•
Paint brush
•
Selection of nylon washers
•
Dylon dye
•
Matching thread
• • •

**2** Paint the styrofoam balls with acrylic paint and dye the nylon washers following the manufacturer's instructions. Leave to dry.

Use this piece to sew ends together

**4** Sew up the bound-off edges, then using the long piece of yarn from where you cast on, sew both ends together to form a circle, hiding the seam under a washer.

**3** Stuff a styrofoam ball bead into the knitted tube, then thread on a washer. Continue in this way until the tube is filled.

This exquisite gilt-edged brooch and earrings borrow from the colors, materials, and contrasting *Sumptuous* textures used in *silk jewelry* traditional Indian textiles. The fabric is decorated with rich machine embroidery, then embellished with tiny handsewn beads.

Stitching on back of brooch

## Materials

• • •

Piece of silk fabric at least 4 × 8 inches

•

Craft-weight interfacing

•

Sewing machine

•

Selection of machine embroidery threads including a gold metallic and a shaded thread

•

Selection of small beads

•

No. 2 round cane

•

1 large bead

•

Needle

•

Fine copper wire

•

Pliers

•

Thin cardboard

•

Fusible webbing

•

Brooch finding

•

Ear wires

•

2 tiny shells

• • •

Interfacing

12mm (½ in)

**1** Cut two pieces of silk fabric and one piece of craft-weight interfacing each about ½ inch bigger than the finished brooch, which will be 3 inches square. Layer them together, then set your sewing machine to straight stitch, and outline the shape of the brooch and an inner square. The outlines can be drawn in pencil or chalk prior to stitching, if necessary.

**2** To create the gold outlines, first wind the metallic thread onto the bobbin, bypassing the tension mechanism by taking the thread through the hole in the bobbin case. Thread the top of the machine with shaded thread. Using straight stitch and working on the back of the brooch, sew several lines around the inner square (the design will come out on the front of the brooch).

**3** The star motif is "drawn" with free machine embroidery, for which you will have to drop or cover the feed dog, according to the machine handbook. This allows the fabric to move freely, enabling you to "draw" with the machine. Replace the

normal sewing foot with a
darning foot, thread with your
chosen color and slacken the
top tension. Stitch the outline
of the star shape, then fill it in,
shading with a different color if
required.

Open zigzag stitches

**4** Trim the fabric to within
$1/12$ inch of the outer stitching.
Return the machine to normal
stitching and, using a close
zigzag stitch, sew over the raw
edges for a neat finish. More
open zigzag stitches in a
different color add interest.
Finish the thread ends.

**5** Decorate the outer edge with
small beads handsewn in place.
Overstitch pieces of cane in
position to outline the inner
square and star motif, adding
more beads as decorative detail.
The large bead at the bottom of
the brooch is attached with fine
copper wire twisted into a loop
with pliers, then joined to one
of the small beads already
stitched to the outer edge.

**6** To stiffen the brooch, cut a
piece of cardboard and a piece
of fusible web to the correct
size, then cut a piece of fabric
$1/4$ inch bigger than these.

Place the fusible web on top of
the cardboard, then center the
fabric on top of this. Fold the
fabric around the cardboard,
then iron in place following the
manufacturer's instructions.
Sew the brooch finding in
place, then whip the completed
backing to the brooch to finish.

Wire threaded with beads

Use pliers to loop wire

Machine embroidery

**7** The earrings are made using the
same techniques. Attach the
ear wires and shells with
twisted wire.

# *Richness from rags* This looks like

the work of a master couturier. In fact, the brooch is made from scraps of fabric and thread, layered between hot-water-soluble fabric and vinyl, then richly decorated, while the earrings are made from embroidered felt bases.

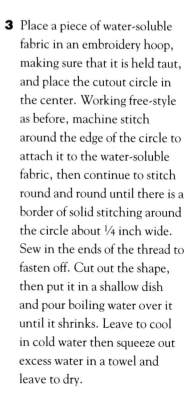

## Materials
• • •
Scraps of silk fabric and threads
•
Hot-water-soluble fabric
•
Vinyl
•
Sewing machine
•
Selection of machine embroidery threads
•
Scissors
•
Embroidery hoop
•
Selection of tiny beads
•
Gold jeweler's wire
•
Pliers
•
Embroider's goldwork wire
•
Superglue
•
Brooch pin
•
Small felt square
•
Selection of larger beads (for drops)
•
Ear wires
• • •

**1** Cut out tiny pieces of brightly colored silk and embroidery threads and put them on top of a piece of hot-water-soluble fabric. Pin a piece of vinyl on top of this, creating a sandwich.

**2** Drop or cover the feed dog on your sewing machine, according to the handbook, allowing the fabric to move freely. Use a darning foot and thread the machine with a different color top and bottom. Loosen the spool tension. Machine embroider together in a freehand style, then cut out a circle. This will form the brooch.

**3** Place a piece of water-soluble fabric in an embroidery hoop, making sure that it is held taut, and place the cutout circle in the center. Working free-style as before, machine stitch around the edge of the circle to attach it to the water-soluble fabric, then continue to stitch round and round until there is a border of solid stitching around the circle about ¼ inch wide. Sew in the ends of the thread to fasten off. Cut out the shape, then put it in a shallow dish and pour boiling water over it until it shrinks. Leave to cool in cold water then squeeze out excess water in a towel and leave to dry.

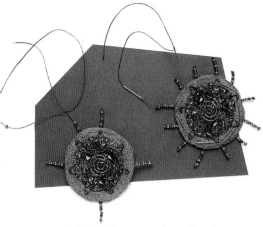

**6** Stitch up and down each heart from side to side until the felt is completely covered. Stitch around the edges again to strengthen. Cut out the shapes and simmer them in a saucepan of water for about 5 minutes. Cool in cold water, squeeze out the excess water in a towel, and leave to dry.

**4** Thread strings of tiny beads in varying lengths and use to decorate the outer edge of the brooch. Take the thread back through all but the very last bead in each string and stitch in place so that the strings radiate out. Make a coil of gold wire with pliers and stitch it to the center, then stitch small pieces of goldwork wire around the edge with beads scattered in between. Glue or stitch the brooch pin in position.

*Simmering in water gives firm finish*

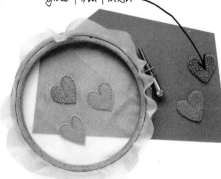

**5** Cut three heart shapes from felt, making them slightly larger than the required size. Set a piece of water-soluble fabric tightly in an embroidery hoop and, with the sewing machine set for free-style embroidery as before, stitch each heart to the fabric around the edges.

**7** To make the drop for the brooch, cut a piece of wire to the required length. Thread on some beads and use pliers to bend both ends of the wire to form a hook. Make a hole in the top of one heart and push a hooked end of wire through. Use pliers to close the hook and secure the heart. Make a hole in the bottom of the brooch and secure the other end of the wire in the same way.

**8** Use pliers to make a decorative wire coil for the bottom of each earring, threading a bead onto the top of each and then bending to form a hook. Cut two smaller pieces of wire, thread on some beads, and use pliers to make hooks at each end. Make a hole in the top and bottom of the two remaining hearts and attach the coils to the bottom and the beaded wire to the top, closing the hooks as before. To finish, attach ear wires and close the hooks to secure.

# ■ ■ ■
# INSPIRATIONS

**Rich fabrics and yarns and ornate embroidery can be used imaginatively to create original and witty pieces of jewelry, as shown here.**

**1 & 2** Vividly colored necklaces using plain or striped beads made from hand-rolled wool felt. *Victoria Brown*

**3** Hand-ruched felt flower brooches. *Victoria Brown*

**4** Made in the same way as rag rugs, these earrings and brooch use T-shirt scraps for fabric. *Lizzie Reakes*

**5 & 6** Witty brooches crafted from fabric to create pea-pod and carrot designs, with painted pearls for peas. *Deirdre Hawken*

**7** Beaded and embroidered neck-piece inspired by Islamic tiles. *Janice Gilmore*

**8** Opulent machine-embroidered brooch. *Judy Clayton*

**9** This cleverly constructed bow tie traps scraps of silk between layers of net. *Susie Freeman*

FaBRIC &
EMBROIDERY

# PaPER

- - -

## ROLLED-PAPER BEADS

- - -

## MEDITERRANEAN MAGIC

- - -

## PAPIER-MÂCHÉ PANEL BRACELET

- - -

## DRAMATIC PAPER AND PASTE EARRINGS

- - -

## HAND-CRAFTED PAPER BROOCH

- - -

## QUILLED FILIGREE JEWELRY

- - -

## ORIGAMI FAN JEWELRY

# 3

## PaPER

# Paper

■ ■ ■ **Paper is superb for making jewelry, as it is so light and versatile. Paper is believed to have been invented by the Chinese, who are also credited with the first use of papier-mâché. Paper looks great when simply shaped or folded, but its chameleon-like qualities enable it to imitate other materials.**

When painted, paper can resemble sheet metal or wood, but it has the advantage of being very light. Shredded and steeped in water, it can be layered over various "frames" or pressed into molds to take on new shapes – as in the craft called papier mâché, which was popular in Britain and the United States during the 19th century.

Paper's other great asset is that it is one of the cheapest materials available – it's even free if you recycle it, which makes it the perfect material for these ecologically aware times.

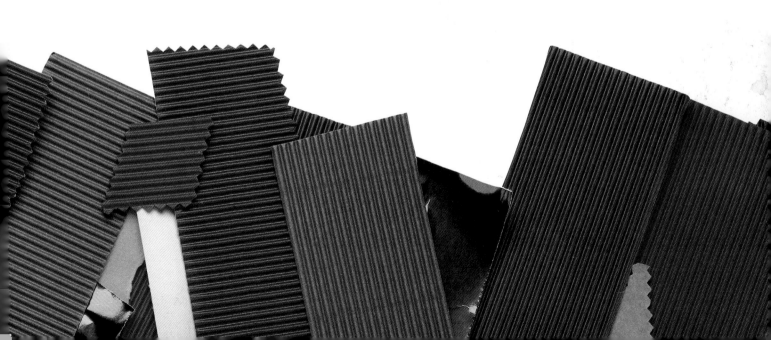

If you are interested in making jewelry using metals or wood but cannot afford the tools and raw materials, paper can be used to make convincing lookalikes. It takes a little practice to perfect the techniques, but if you make a mistake at least you haven't wasted a great deal of money.

Origami and papier-mâché are both well-established crafts in their own right and useful techniques for the jewelry designer to learn. Laminating is a newer process that involves heat-sealing paper with plastic to produce durable, strong shapes with flat, shiny surfaces. Laminating machines are expensive, but your local stationery store, will probably do the job for you for a small charge. Lamination can be done before or after decoration and creates more opportunities for paper jewelry designs. ■ ■ ■

Beads are available in a wide variety of materials. The ones here

resemble fine china,

# *Rolled paper beads* but they are made

from tightly rolled strips of wrapping paper and

are as light as a feather. They look exquisite strung

together, and nobody would guess they are

just paper!

## Materials
• • •
Sheets of
wrapping paper –
1 or 2 patterned,
2 black, 1 silver
•
Gold quilling paper
(for tiny beads)
•
Pencil
•
Metal ruler
•
Craft knife or
scissors
•
Quilling tool or thin
knitting needle
•
White glue
•
Needle
•
Strong thread
•
Head pins
•
Pliers
•
Ear wires
•
Spray varnish
(optional)
• • •

**1** Using a pencil, mark the long edge of a sheet of patterned paper on the wrong side with the widths of beads required – we made 11 × ¾ inch, 13 × ½ inch, and 13 × 1 inch. Mark the same widths on the opposite edge, then draw parallel lines between the marks. Cut out the strips using a craft knife and metal ruler or scissors. Cut all but two of the strips in half (leave two ½-inch strips uncut to make the earrings). Take six strips of gold quilling paper and cut each into eight equal lengths.

**2** Using a quilling tool or your fingers and a thin knitting needle, roll a strip of paper tightly to make a cylinder-shaped bead, leaving a hole in the center big enough to fit the thread through. Glue the end of the paper with as little glue as possible and hold the bead for a moment while the glue sets. Roll up the rest of the strips, gluing as before, then roll up the quilling paper to make tiny gold beads.

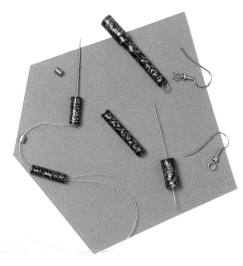

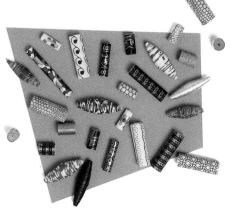

**4** To make the black and silver oval beads, cut a 12-inch square of wrapping paper in each color. On the wrong side of each square, mark one edge at 1-inch intervals, then mark its opposite edge ½ inch in and then at 1-inch intervals. Draw lines between the marks, as shown, and cut out the elongated triangles, discarding the two at the edge as they will not be the correct shape. Cut a 6 × 12-inch rectangle of black paper into straight ¼ × 12-inch strips.

**6** Different types of paper create exciting effects when rolled up to form beads. Try recycling birthday and holiday wrapping papers or even old magazines. Creases can be ironed out using a low heat setting, and if you don't like the final effect, you can always paint the beads with nail polish or enamel.

**3** Make an earring by threading one fat ½-inch bead and one 1-inch bead onto a head pin. Use pliers to turn a loop at the top of the pin and then attach an ear wire to this. Make the other earring in the same way. Thread the remaining beads on strong thread to make a necklace, using them in the following order – 1 inch, ½ inch, ¾ inch, ½ inch. Repeat to the end, threading tiny gold beads between each paper bead. Spray with varnish, if desired, to make them last longer.

**5** Lay a silver triangle over a black one so that a narrow edge of black can be seen. Starting from the wide end, roll the two strips together as before and glue the ends in place. Roll the straight black strips up tightly to form small beads to use between the ovals. Make the beads into earrings and necklace as before.

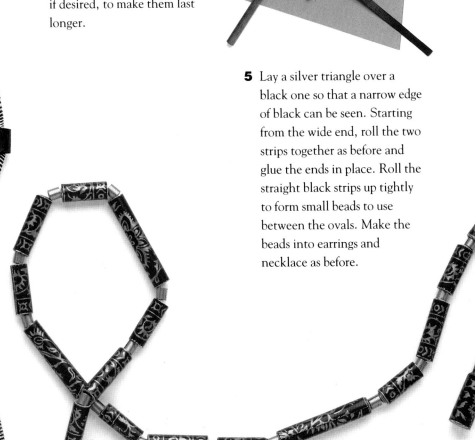

# Mediterranean *magic*

The craft of papier-mâché is simple to master and can be used to create professional-looking jewelry for very little cost. The beads that make up this stylish necklace were created using the layering technique then painted in bright colors inspired by Mediterranean china. They can be made in any size and strung into necklaces or wired to make earrings.

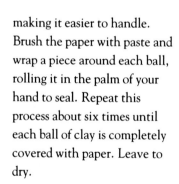

## Materials
▪ ▪ ▪
Modeling clay
▪
Newspaper
▪
Wallpaper paste
(with white glue)
▪
Paint brushes
▪
Craft knife or
sharp kitchen knife
▪
White glue
▪
Paints in colors of
choice
▪
Permanent marker
pen
▪
Varnish
▪
Darning needle
▪
Nylon thread
▪
Clasp (optional)
▪ ▪ ▪

**1** Roll the clay into balls, remembering that, when finished, they will be slightly bigger because of the papier-mâché. Roll enough for the length of necklace you want. Tear the newspaper into neat strips, about $5/8 \times 1\frac{1}{2}$ inches. Mix the wallpaper paste following the manufacturer's instructions, but use hot water – this seeps into the paper, making it easier to handle. Brush the paper with paste and wrap a piece around each ball, rolling it in the palm of your hand to seal. Repeat this process about six times until each ball of clay is completely covered with paper. Leave to dry.

Use a sharp blade for a clean cut

**2** Using a craft knife or sharp kitchen knife, cut each bead in half. Carefully remove the clay from the middle; then glue the paper halves back together with strong adhesive. If necessary, wrap another layer of paper over each bead to conceal the seam. Leave to dry.

**3** Decorate the beads in colors and design of your choice. If you are using a light base color, cover the beads with a coat of white latex or gesso first to prevent newsprint from showing through. The design detail has been added to these beads with a black, fine-pointed permanent marker pen. Leave to dry, then finish with a coat of varnish.

*Pierce beads with needle*

**4** To make into a necklace, use a darning needle threaded with strong nylon thread, such as fishing line, to string the beads to the desired length. Finish with a clasp or knot securely.

# *Dramatic paper and paste earrings*

Bright glass or plastic "jewels" combine with simple papier mâché shapes in dazzling colors to produce a stunning pair of earrings and a necklace that are right up to the minute. Foil candy wrappers form a golden halo around the stones.

## Materials

* * *

Selection of glass or plastic jewel stones

Cardboard

Pencil

Scissors

Wallpaper paste

Newspaper

Foil candy wrappers

White paint for undercoat

Poster paint

White glue

Pierced earring backs and butterfly fastenings

Darning needle

Short eye pins

Varnish

* * *

**2** Mix the wallpaper paste with hot water, following the manufacturer's instructions, then tear the newspaper into small, even pieces. Cover the larger pieces of cardboard with three layers of pasted newspaper. Enclose the smaller pieces in foil candy wrappers, gluing to secure. Leave to dry.

**1** Place your chosen jewel stones on top of the cardboard and draw a circle or a square around each one, depending on the shape of the stones. For each jewel stone, cut out one piece of cardboard $1/12$ inch larger than the stone and one piece $1/8$ inch larger.

**3** Paint the newspaper-covered pieces with white paint to prevent the newsprint from showing through. Leave to dry, then paint with two or three coats of your chosen color.

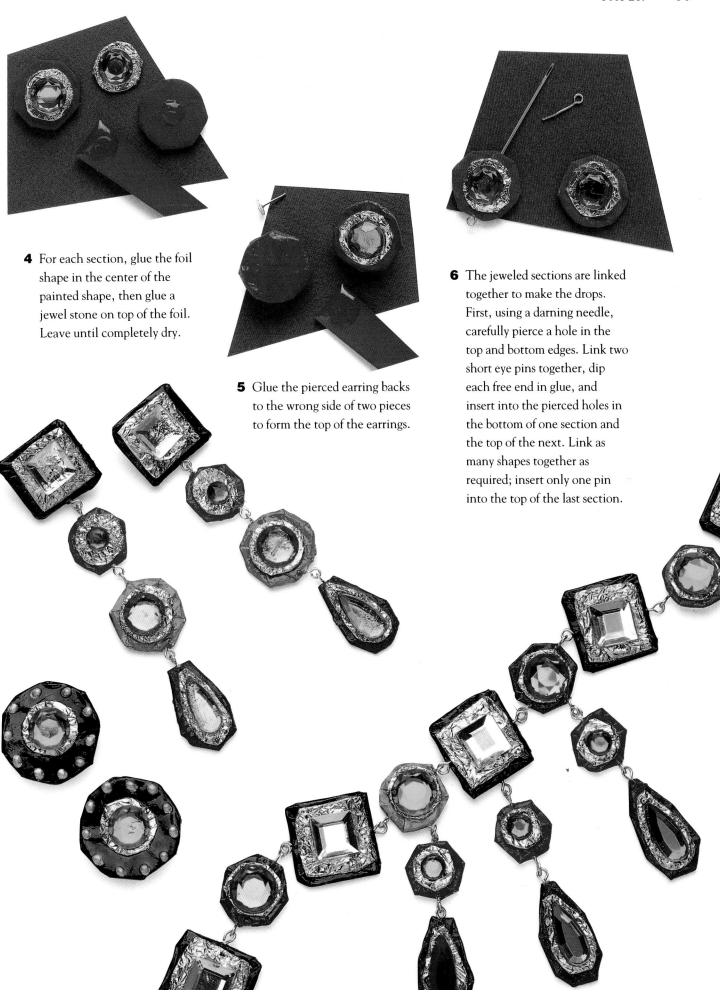

**4** For each section, glue the foil shape in the center of the painted shape, then glue a jewel stone on top of the foil. Leave until completely dry.

**5** Glue the pierced earring backs to the wrong side of two pieces to form the top of the earrings.

**6** The jeweled sections are linked together to make the drops. First, using a darning needle, carefully pierce a hole in the top and bottom edges. Link two short eye pins together, dip each free end in glue, and insert into the pierced holes in the bottom of one section and the top of the next. Link as many shapes together as required; insert only one pin into the top of the last section.

# Papier-mâché panel bracelet

Paper and paint are the basic materials needed to make this unusual bracelet. A cardboard template is strengthened with papier-mâché layers, then decorated with architecturally inspired motifs. The use of bronze and old gold metallic paints on a black background gives the bracelet a wonderfully rich finish.

Template

## Materials

• • •

Cardboard
•
Tape measure
•
Craft knife or scissors
•
Pencil
•
Ruler
•
Newspaper
•
Wallpaper paste
•
Black latex paint
•
Gold acrylic paint
•
Metallic acrylic paint
•
Paint brushes
•
Varnish
•
Leather hole punch
•
Round elastic
•
Superglue

• • •

**1** Measure your wrist loosely to find the length required. Using a craft knife or scissors, cut a piece of cardboard this length × 2 inches wide, then divide it into seven or eight sections, marking each with a pencil line. Cut out the sections and draw pointed shapes along the top and bottom edges of one piece. Cut out around the points and use this section as a template for cutting out the remaining sections.

**2** Tear newspaper into small, neat strips, then mix the wallpaper paste, following the manufacturer's instructions. Brush the paper strips with paste and use to cover the cardboard shapes. The number of layers will depend on the thickness of the cardboard. You need to end up with hard, rigid pieces that won't bend in wear. Leave each layer of paper to dry completely before applying the next.

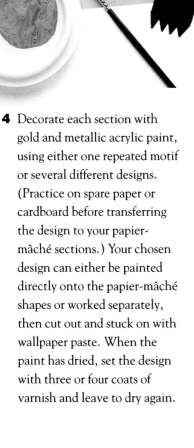

**3** Paint each section with black latex paint.

**4** Decorate each section with gold and metallic acrylic paint, using either one repeated motif or several different designs. (Practice on spare paper or cardboard before transferring the design to your papier-mâché sections.) Your chosen design can either be painted directly onto the papier-mâché shapes or worked separately, then cut out and stuck on with wallpaper paste. When the paint has dried, set the design with three or four coats of varnish and leave to dry again.

**5** Use the leather hole punch to make three holes along each side of each section. Thread elastic through the holes, weaving it over and under as illustrated. When all the sections have been threaded on to the elastic, check for fit and then secure with neat double knots. Add a dot of glue to anchor each knot.

**Variation** To bead the bracelet, make holes along the top of each section. Thread beads onto a head pin, trim, and use pliers to make a loop at the top of the head pin. Push a jump ring through each hole. Attach bead strings to each jump ring, then close the jump rings with pliers.

# Hand-crafted

# paper brooch
Simple shapes, highlighted with gold and foil, are cleverly combined to make this impressive paper brooch. Inspired by the decorative patterns, shapes, and colors used by ancient civilizations, the brooch is put together with ingenious use of modern technology and is strikingly contemporary in style.

## Materials
• • •

Sheet of white typing paper
•
Smaller pieces of blue and purple paper of a similar weight
•
Purple foil paper
•
Gold foil (from candy wrappers)
•
Gold spray paint
•
Small sponge
•
Black paint
•
Colored inks
•
Craft knife or scissors
•
Gold marker pen
•
Soldering iron
•
Strong glue
•
Transparent self-adhesive plastic
•
Glass paper
•
Brooch back

• • •

**2** With a hot soldering iron, singe the edges of the main shape and the narrow strip to soften and gently curve them.

*Use craft knife to make slits*

**1** Spray one side of the white typing paper with metallic gold paint and, when dry, lightly sponge the other side using black paint and paint in detail with colored inks. Leave until completely dry, then cut out a shape using a craft knife or sharp scissors. Highlight the sponged design with gold marker pen. Cut a narrow strip from the blue paper plus small triangles from the purple paper.

**3** Lay the narrow strip on top of the main piece and mark where to cut the slots for the narrow strip (see the finished pieces for a guide to positioning these). Carefully cut two slits for each slot, then edge the cuts using gold marker pen.

**4** Tear a strip of gold foil from a candy wrapper and glue it in position along the narrow blue strip. Highlight the edges of each purple triangle with gold marker pen. Glue pieces of purple foil to the triangles.

**6** The brooch can be made more robust either by laminating it (try a stationery or office supply store), or cover it with transparent self-adhesive plastic. Cut two pieces of plastic larger than the finished brooch, peel off the backing, and place the brooch between the pieces, carefully smoothing out any wrinkles. Trim to 1/16 inch all around the shape.

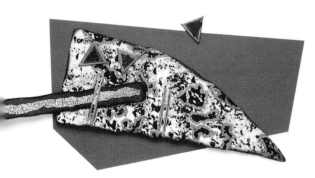

**5** Glue the triangles to the brooch and thread the blue strip through the slots.

**7** Using fine sandpaper, gently roughen up the area of plastic that the brooch back will be attached. Glue the brooch back in position.

Quilling is one of the most popular paper-crafts and is often used for greeting cards

# Quilled filigree jewelry

designs. The shapes produced by quilling look like fine filigree work, which was the inspiration for this sophisticated necklace and matching earrings. The finished pieces look fragile and delicate, but are in fact more robust than they appear.

## Materials

• • •

Black ⅛-inch quilling paper

•

Silver felt-tip pen

•

Quilling tool

•

White glue

•

Spray varnish

•

Large jump rings

•

Bolt ring

•

Ear wires

• • •

**1** Interesting effects can be achieved in quilling by coloring the edge of the paper, particularly if you use metallic ink. To do this, simply run the pen along the edges of each strip of paper. For the necklace, you need color only one edge, as only the front will be seen.

**2** Tear a strip of quilling paper in half. Slip an untorn end of the strip into the quilling tool and turn it to wind up the paper, using your other hand to guide it so it coils evenly. For the coil to lie flat, you need to make sure that each winding lies directly on top of the last. When you reach the end, let the paper go so that it falls off the tool. Anchor the end of the coil in place with a little glue. This motif is called a closed coil.

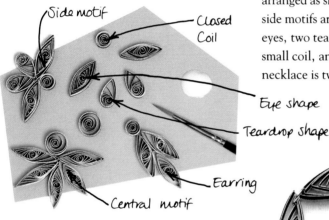

**3** Practice coiling evenly until all the coils made from the same length of paper are the same finished size. To make the necklace, you will need 37 closed coils made from half a strip of paper, five made from a third of a strip, and 30 from a quarter of a strip. For the earrings, you will need six from half a strip and two from a quarter of a strip.

Side motif
Closed Coil
Eye shape
Teardrop shape
Earring
Central motif

**4** Shape one of the half-strip coils by pinching firmly at two points opposite each other on the coil. Make sure you pinch both points at the same time so that the beginning of the coil stays in the center to form an eye shape. Repeat for all the half-strip coils. Take a third-strip coil and pinch at one point to form a teardrop. Repeat for three of these, leaving one as it is.

**5** Stick the shapes together using the tiniest amount of glue, making sure that all the shapes for the necklace have the silver edge facing up. The central motif is made from five eyes and the round, third-strip coil arranged as shown. The two side motifs are made from two eyes, two teardrops, and one small coil, and the rest of the necklace is two eyes and two

coils. Each earring consists of three eyes and a small coil. When the glue has dried, spray the pieces with varnish.

**6** To make the necklace, link the motifs together using jump rings. As the paper is so fine and can easily slip through, seal the joint in each ring with a dab of glue. Attach a bolt ring to the last jump ring on one side. The earrings also use a jump ring to link the motif to the ear wire.

This unusual jewelry is inspired by traditional origami techniques, and the paper certainly has

# Origami fan jewelry

a Japanese feel with its brilliantly colored flowers on a black background. Once you have mastered the art, experiment with different papers – marbled and foil papers work particularly well – to produce original finished pieces.

## Materials

• • •

Wrapping paper or origami paper

•

Scissors

•

White glue

•

Eye pins

•

Ear wires

•

Brooch pin

• • •

**1** Cut two 4-inch squares and four 2-inch squares from the paper. With the wrong side of the paper facing up, fold each square in half diagonally and crease, then fold in half again on the opposite diagonal and crease. This marks the center point (where the diagonals cross).

**2** Keeping the wrong side facing you, fold all four points of a 2-inch square to the center point. Crease each fold sharply. Turn the folded square so that a point is at the top, then fold both side points across to meet the center line, creating a kite shape. Crease sharply.

Eye pin

**3** Fold the shape in half along the center line, enclosing the previous folds, to form half an earring. Fold a second small square in the same way as the first, then glue an eye pin inside the last fold at the top point so that only the loop of the pin can be seen. Place the two shapes opposite each other with their side points facing, then, overlapping the edges of each shape, tuck the two together.

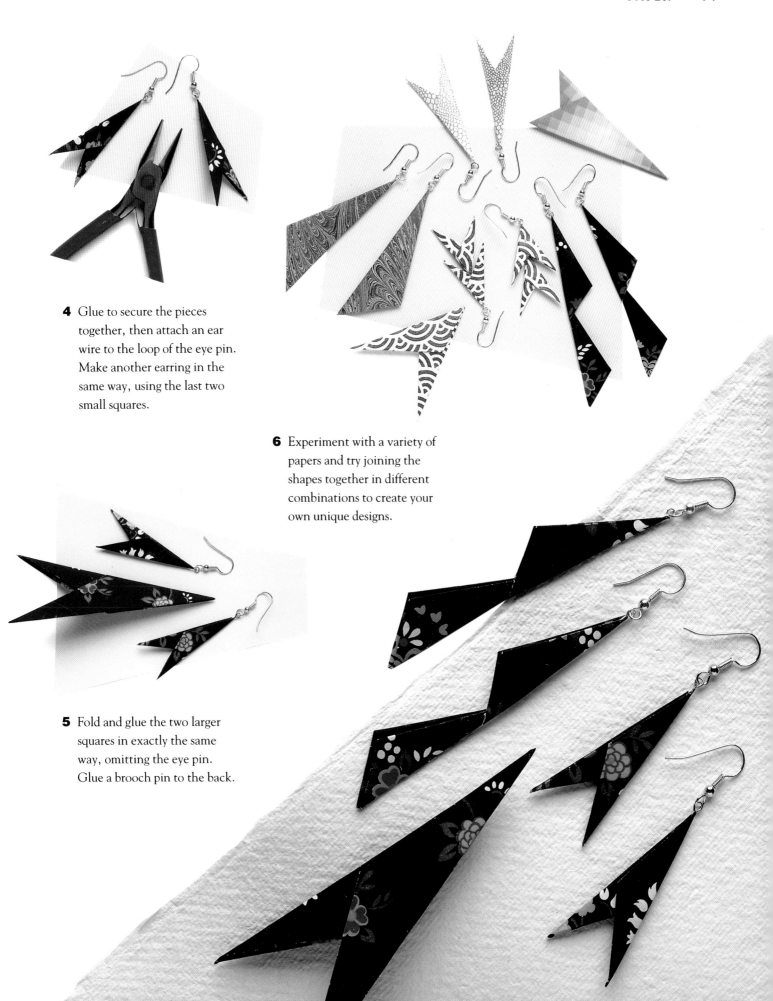

**4** Glue to secure the pieces together, then attach an ear wire to the loop of the eye pin. Make another earring in the same way, using the last two small squares.

**6** Experiment with a variety of papers and try joining the shapes together in different combinations to create your own unique designs.

**5** Fold and glue the two larger squares in exactly the same way, omitting the eye pin. Glue a brooch pin to the back.

## ▪ ▪ ▪
# INSPIRATIONS

**These stunning pieces are a tribute to the versatility of paper and demonstrate the variety of effects that can be achieved using different techniques.**

**1** Tissue paper and wire brooch cleverly painted to look like bark. *Julia Manheim*

**2** Sculpted papier-mâché cone necklace. *Julia Manheim*

**3** Richly decorated papier-mâché earrings and brooch. *Yanina Temple*

**4** Cheerful papier-mâché earrings and brooch made using a mold. *Mandy Nash*

**5** Laminated paper brooches. *Hammie Tappenden*

**6** Papier-mâché necklace shaped to look like pebbles. *Anastasia Chao*

**7** Wooden bead necklace with brilliantly colored papier-mâché drops. *Deirdre Hawken*

**8** Layered papier-mâché bangles inspired by Hungarian folk art. *Jeannell Kolkman*

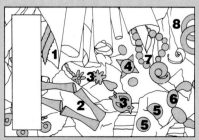

PaPER

# CLaY&
# PLaSTIC

• • •

**VALENTINE HEARTS**

• • •

**CONTEMPORARY CHIC**

• • •

**LOUNGE LIZARD**

• • •

**INCA-INSPIRED NECKLACE**

• • •

**SEASHELL BARETTE AND
EARRINGS**

• • •

**HARLEQUIN HEARTS**

• • •

**ZIGZAG COPPER JEWELRY**

• • •

**MARBLED BEAD NECKLACE**

# 4

# CLAY & PLASTIC

# Clay and plastic

■ ■ ■ Today's easy-to-use synthetic modeling clays have made it possible to produce jewelry that imitates fine porcelain at home. Their big advantage is that they set hard at low temperatures, and some even air-dry, whereas traditional ceramics need to be fired at temperatures beyond the capabilities of the home oven. Another plus point is that the finished articles are much more robust and less prone to breakage.

Strips of polymer clay in different colors can be kneaded together to create marbled effects, and it is possible to design and make your own millefiori beads (see page 32) with a little practice. Polymer clay is pliable enough to be pressed into molds, rolled into beads, or rolled out flat and cut into shapes with pastry cutters or a craft knife. After firing your

pieces in a low oven (approximately 250°F), you can decorate them with jewel stones, metallic powders, and acrylic paints to create stunning, realistic pieces of jewelry. Air-drying clays are available only in natural, white, or terracotta, but otherwise they can be molded and decorated in the same way as polymer clay.

Meltable plastic is a fascinating new craft material which is available in a variety of brightly colored plain and metallic strips. When heated, either in hot water or in the oven, it magically becomes soft and pliable, allowing you to mold or cut it to any shape you like. As it cools, it regains its rigidity, but can be reheated and softened so you can add more pieces to your design. When you have finished working your design, simply drop it into cold water for about five minutes to set it firm. It will be ready to wear after a couple of hours. ■ ■ ■

# Valentine hearts

These heart earrings and brooch are made from a modern air-drying clay that gives a wonderful ceramic finish without the need for an expensive kiln. They are simple to make using pastry cutters, and the finished pieces look good enough for either day or evening wear.

## Materials
• • •
Small amount of air-drying clay such as Das
•
Rolling pin
•
Heart-shaped cutters (small, medium, and large)
•
Teardrop-shaped cutter
•
Gilt head or eye pins
•
Wire cutters
•
Pliers
•
Small paint brush
•
Superglue
•
Fine sandpaper or emery board
•
White polymer latex or gesso
•
Pierced or clip earring findings
•
Brooch pin
•
Red liquid acrylic enamel paint
•
Gold paint
•
Jump rings
•
Varnish
•
Length of gilt chain
• • •

**1** To make the earrings, knead a small amount of clay in your hands until it is soft and pliable. Roll out with a rolling pin on a nonporous surface (marble or a ceramic tile are both ideal) until approximately ¼ inch thick. Cut out two hearts with a medium cutter and two teardrops.

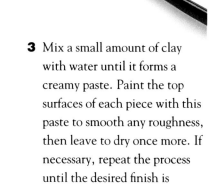

**2** Take four eye or head pins; if using head pins, snip off the flat "head" from each one with wire cutters, then turn a loop at one end with pliers. Trim and insert carefully into the bottom of each heart and the top of each teardrop. Eye pins will only need trimming. Leave the clay to dry hard.

**3** Mix a small amount of clay with water until it forms a creamy paste. Paint the top surfaces of each piece with this paste to smooth any roughness, then leave to dry once more. If necessary, repeat the process until the desired finish is achieved.

**4** Check that the pins are secure; if not, dip the ends in glue and reinsert into the holes. When they are dry, use a very fine sandpaper or emery board to smooth the outer edges.

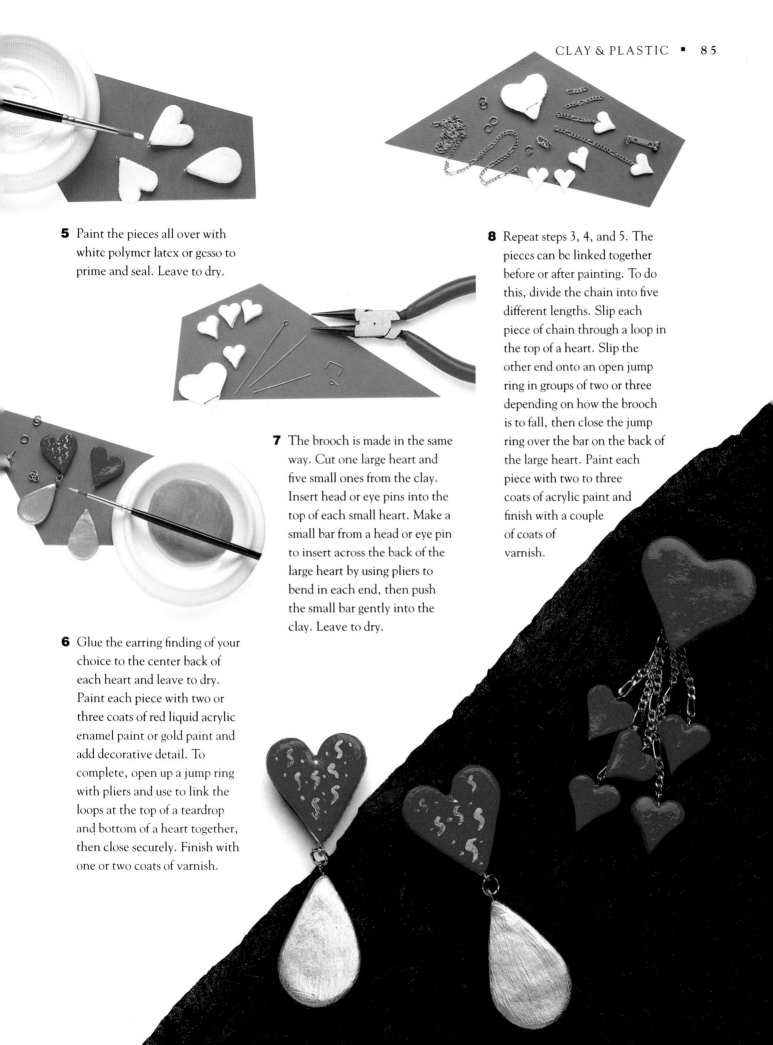

**5** Paint the pieces all over with white polymer latex or gesso to prime and seal. Leave to dry.

**6** Glue the earring finding of your choice to the center back of each heart and leave to dry. Paint each piece with two or three coats of red liquid acrylic enamel paint or gold paint and add decorative detail. To complete, open up a jump ring with pliers and use to link the loops at the top of a teardrop and bottom of a heart together, then close securely. Finish with one or two coats of varnish.

**7** The brooch is made in the same way. Cut one large heart and five small ones from the clay. Insert head or eye pins into the top of each small heart. Make a small bar from a head or eye pin to insert across the back of the large heart by using pliers to bend in each end, then push the small bar gently into the clay. Leave to dry.

**8** Repeat steps 3, 4, and 5. The pieces can be linked together before or after painting. To do this, divide the chain into five different lengths. Slip each piece of chain through a loop in the top of a heart. Slip the other end onto an open jump ring in groups of two or three depending on how the brooch is to fall, then close the jump ring over the bar on the back of the large heart. Paint each piece with two to three coats of acrylic paint and finish with a couple of coats of varnish.

These jazzy earrings are fine examples of what can be achieved with polymer modeling clay. They are made from two contrasting colors, and the final design is added in acrylic paint. The

# *Contemporary chic*

finished pieces are extremely stylish.

## Materials
· · ·
2 packs of polymer clay, in contrasting colors
·
Rolling pin
·
Small piece of paper or cardboard for template
·
Craft knife
·
Thin gilt wire
·
Wire cutters
·
Pliers
·
Jump rings
·
Ear wires
·
Acrylic paint in 3 colors
·
Gold paint
·
Paint brushes
·
Varnish
· · ·

*Don't roll clay too thin*

**1** Knead the first color of clay with your hands until it is soft and pliable. Roll out with a rolling pin on a flat, non-porous surface (marble or a ceramic tile is ideal) until it is ¼ inch thick.

**2** Draw your shape on paper or cardboard and make a template for the main piece. Place it on the clay and cut around it carefully, using a craft knife. Cut out smaller pieces for the hanging sections.

**3** Cut the wire into short lengths with wire cutters, then using pliers, make ten hoops as shown. Gently press them into the clay, three on the main piece and one on each of the hanging sections, as illustrated.

Conceal hoops with small pieces of clay

**4** Knead and roll out the second pack of clay, as before. Cut out small pieces and use to cover the hoops. Press gently but firmly to make sure that the hoops are held securely in place, then bake in the oven on low heat, following the instructions on the package. Leave to cool.

**5** Open the jump rings with pliers and use to link the hoops on the hanging sections to those at the base of the main piece. Use another jump ring to link the hoop at the top to an ear wire.

**6** Use acrylic paints and gold paint to decorate the clay with your chosen design. Finish with a coat of varnish, paying particular attention to the areas where the hoops emerge.

**Variation** You can make a pendant in the same way, but pierce top holes in the pieces with a needle before baking. Attach to a neck chain with jump rings.

This brooch was inspired by the elegant animal jewelry of the

# *Lounge lizard* 1940s, which was made

fashionable by the Duchess

of Windsor and has recently been enjoying a revival. It can be made

in just a couple of hours from modeling clay and

inexpensive jewel stones, yet it looks remarkably authentic

and has more than a touch of Forties' sophistication.

**1** Either trace or photocopy the lizard template (direct) then cut around the shape so you have a paper pattern. Roll out the clay with a rolling pin until it is about ⅛ inch thick – no thinner, or the jewel stones may pierce right through it. To make the clay more malleable, keep warming it in your hands while rolling. Place the paper pattern on top of the clay.

## Materials

• • •

Tracing paper and pencil

Block of gray Fimo or similar polymer clay

Rolling pin

Craft knife

Jewel stones, including 2 red or green ones for the eyes

Aluminum foil

Baking sheet

Fimo silver powder

Fimo varnish

Epoxy glue

Tweezers

Brooch pin

• • •

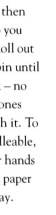

**2** Cut around the paper pattern with a craft knife. Cut each foot out as a solid block, scoring the surface of the Fimo to mark out the claws. Remove the paper, then cut out the claws, taking care that they are not too thin or they may break.

**3** Start positioning the jewel stones in the Fimo, pressing them gently into place. It is easier if you place your first row centrally down the lizard's backbone and then work outward. If the clay is the correct thickness, the stones should sink about halfway down – any farther, and it may break in delicate areas.

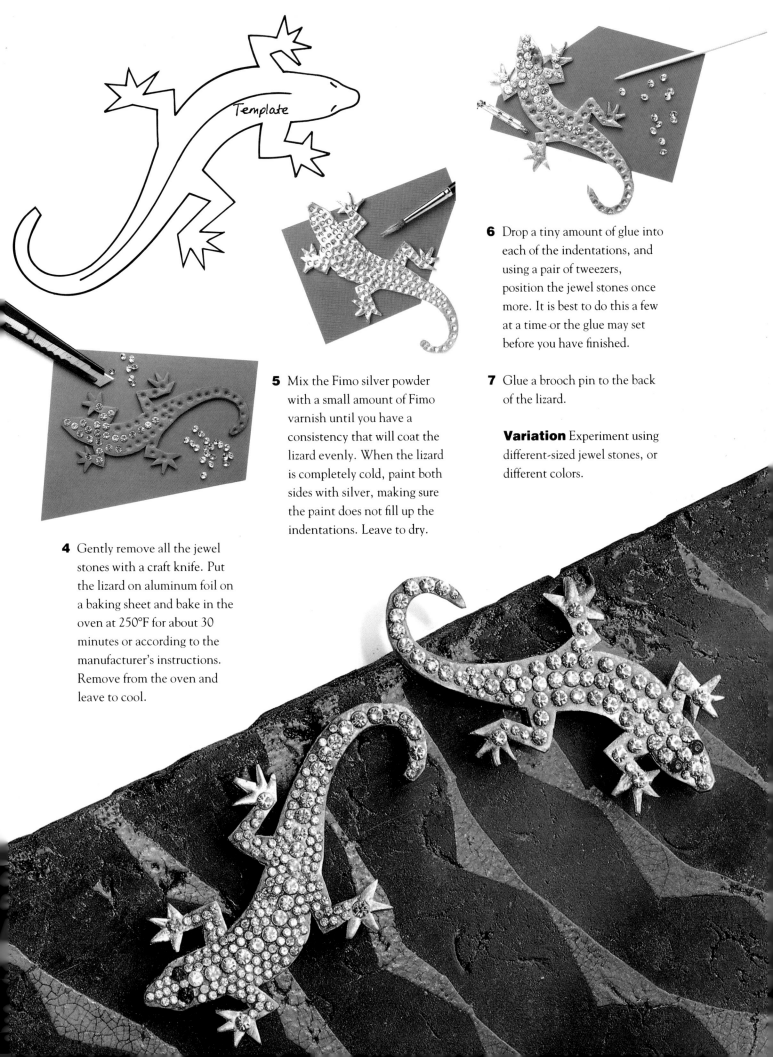

Template

**5** Mix the Fimo silver powder with a small amount of Fimo varnish until you have a consistency that will coat the lizard evenly. When the lizard is completely cold, paint both sides with silver, making sure the paint does not fill up the indentations. Leave to dry.

**6** Drop a tiny amount of glue into each of the indentations, and using a pair of tweezers, position the jewel stones once more. It is best to do this a few at a time or the glue may set before you have finished.

**7** Glue a brooch pin to the back of the lizard.

**Variation** Experiment using different-sized jewel stones, or different colors.

**4** Gently remove all the jewel stones with a craft knife. Put the lizard on aluminum foil on a baking sheet and bake in the oven at 250°F for about 30 minutes or according to the manufacturer's instructions. Remove from the oven and leave to cool.

Inspiration for this striking necklace came from the ancient Inca civilization of South America. The designer wanted to create something

# *Inca-inspired*
# *necklace*

with a look of the past, using Friendly Plastic, one of today's newest modeling materials. This medium softens on contact with heat, enabling you to mold it however you want.

Pieces bond together after heating

## Materials
· · ·
Friendly Plastic strips in mottled gold, silver, and bronze
·
Scissors
·
Pinking shears
·
Baking sheet
·
Darning needle
·
Jump rings
·
Pliers
·
Leather thong
·
Selection of round and tubular beads
·
Crimp end connector (optional)
·
Necklace clasp (optional)
· · ·

**1** Use scissors to cut out nine 1-inch squares in mottled gold. Use pinking shears to cut nine ½ × ¾-inch pieces in silver. Cut out nine narrow strips in bronze with pinking shears, then trim them so that they fit diagonally on the silver pieces, as illustrated.

**2** Lay a silver piece on top of each mottled gold square, then a bronze strip on top of the silver. Transfer to a lightly oiled baking sheet and bake in a preheated oven at 225°F for 1–2 minutes to bond the pieces together. Remove, drop the pieces in cold water, and leave for about 5 minutes, to set.

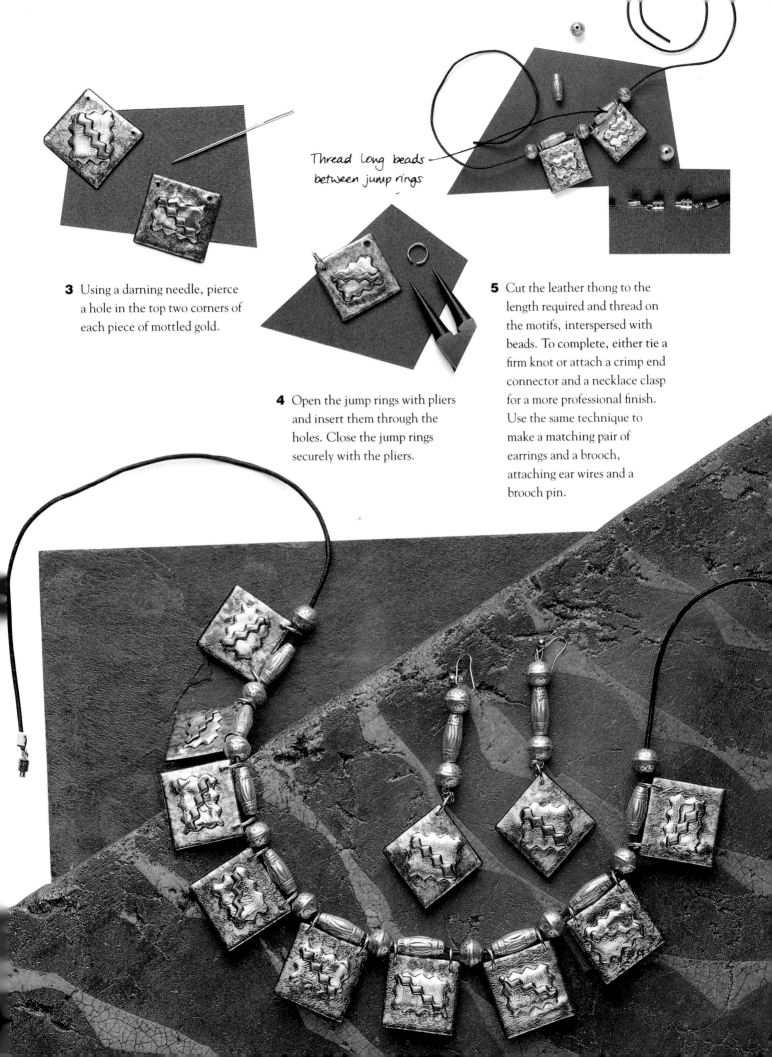

Thread long beads between jump rings

**3** Using a darning needle, pierce a hole in the top two corners of each piece of mottled gold.

**4** Open the jump rings with pliers and insert them through the holes. Close the jump rings securely with the pliers.

**5** Cut the leather thong to the length required and thread on the motifs, interspersed with beads. To complete, either tie a firm knot or attach a crimp end connector and a necklace clasp for a more professional finish. Use the same technique to make a matching pair of earrings and a brooch, attaching ear wires and a brooch pin.

This wonderful barette
and matching earrings
were inspired by summer
days at the seashore. They

# Seashell barette and

# earrings

are perfect examples of
how Friendly Plastic strips
can be molded into
a variety of shapes
and given a three-
dimensional
appearance.

## Materials

Friendly Plastic
strips in silver,
gold, and copper

Barette finding

Scissors

Skewer

Starfish and shell
molds

Selection of jewel
stones – with and
without settings

Superglue

Pierced ear backs
and butterfly
fastenings

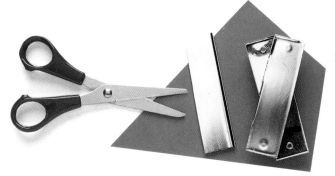

**1** Cut a strip of silver Friendly
Plastic in half and then trim
with scissors to fit the base of
the barette finding. Place in an
oven preheated to 200°F for
about 1 minute to melt the
plastic into the barette.

**2** Place the gold and copper
plastic strips in a pan of hot
water (about 130°F). When
they have softened, take them
out using a skewer or something
similar. Press into the shell-
shaped molds. Set the plastic
by placing the molds in a bowl
of cold water for a few minutes,
then ease the shapes away from
their molds and trim the edges
with a pair of small, sharp
scissors. Place the shells on the
barette base to check the
design.

**3** Build up your design with different-shaped shells made as for step 2. Press the shell shapes in place on the barette base – no glue is required if they are applied to the still-warm plastic. Return it to the oven briefly to soften, if necessary.

**6** Make two more starfish in gold for the earrings. Glue the earring backs in place and apply coordinating jewel stones to finish.

**5** Glue the jewelry settings to the slide, arranging them randomly over the design. Insert the jewel stones into the settings and fold the clips over them to secure firmly.

**4** Soften another strip of gold and press into a starfish mold, as before, trimming the shape with sharp scissors. This final piece will need to be glued in position with superglue.

This delightful heart-shaped jewelry is made from a remarkable material known as shrink-art plastic. It is fine

# Harlequin hearts

enough for the shapes to be cut out using scissors, but when you put it in a barely warm oven, it shrinks like magic, creating smaller and thicker shapes with a brighter, more concentrated design.

## Materials
• • •
2 small sheets or 1 large sheet of shrink-art plastic
▪
Fine sandpaper
▪
Set of heart-shaped rubber stamps featuring different designs
▪
Ink pad with black permanent ink
▪
Permanent-ink felt-tip pens in a variety of colors
▪
Scissors
▪
Heart-shaped hole punch, or an ordinary round hole punch
▪
Baking sheet
▪
Pliers
▪
Jump rings
▪
Ear wires
▪
2 x 16-inch silver chains with clasps
▪
Wire cutters
• • •

**1** Rub one side of the plastic gently all over with sandpaper to give the ink a good surface to cling to. Prime the rubber stamps by tapping them lightly on the ink pad, then print on scrap paper until you get a feel for how much ink you need to use for the best image. You will need 27 hearts altogether to make the necklace, earrings, and bracelet set. Print 27 hearts on the plastic, plus an extra one to use as a test piece. Leave the ink to dry completely: test for dryness by coloring a line on the test piece with one of the colored felt-tip pens – if there is no smearing, the ink is dry.

**2** Color the hearts with felt-tip pens and leave to dry. The color becomes much more intense when the plastic shrinks, so you may like to use the test piece to try out different amounts of color, and bake it before completing the remaining hearts.

**3** Cut out the hearts carefully using scissors, then punch holes at the top and bottom of six hearts for the earrings and on both sides of seven hearts for the necklace. Make one hole at the top of each remaining heart for the bracelet and the bottom of the earrings.

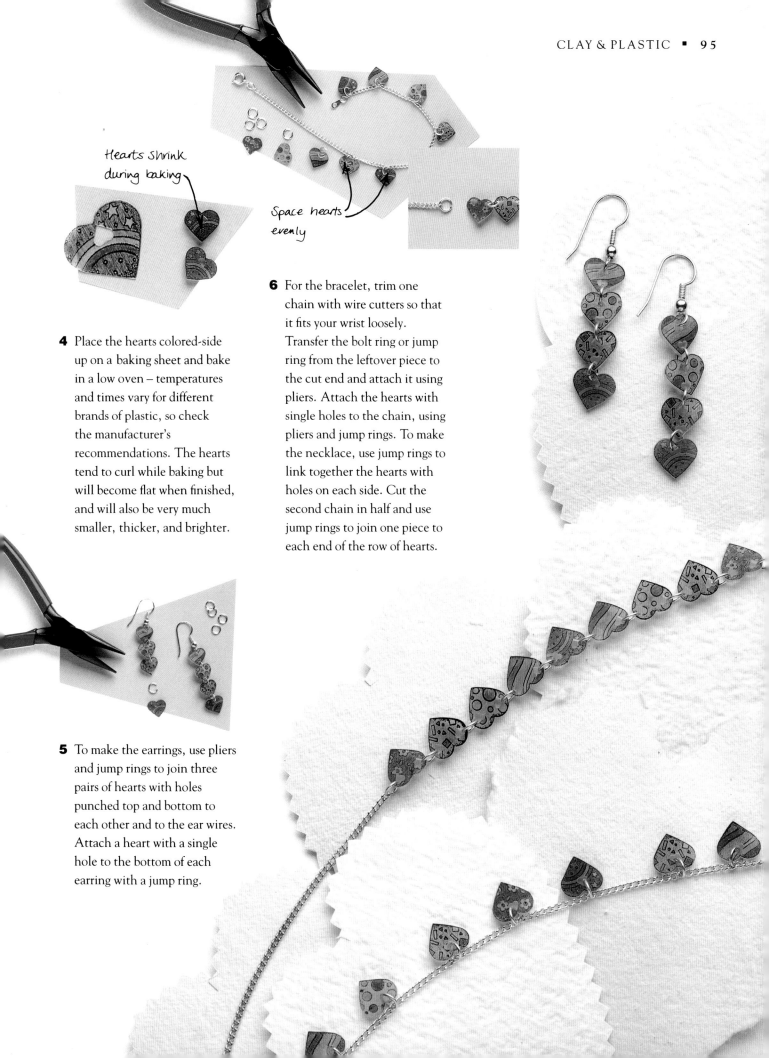

Hearts shrink during baking

Space hearts evenly

**4** Place the hearts colored-side up on a baking sheet and bake in a low oven – temperatures and times vary for different brands of plastic, so check the manufacturer's recommendations. The hearts tend to curl while baking but will become flat when finished, and will also be very much smaller, thicker, and brighter.

**6** For the bracelet, trim one chain with wire cutters so that it fits your wrist loosely. Transfer the bolt ring or jump ring from the leftover piece to the cut end and attach it using pliers. Attach the hearts with single holes to the chain, using pliers and jump rings. To make the necklace, use jump rings to link together the hearts with holes on each side. Cut the second chain in half and use jump rings to join one piece to each end of the row of hearts.

**5** To make the earrings, use pliers and jump rings to join three pairs of hearts with holes punched top and bottom to each other and to the ear wires. Attach a heart with a single hole to the bottom of each earring with a jump ring.

Contrasting materials like copper and plexiglass can be combined for an interesting effect. The

# *Zigzag copper jewelry*

simple shapes that form the basis of these designs are the perfect starting point if you are not experienced in working with "hard" materials.

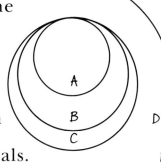

templates

A
B
C
D
E

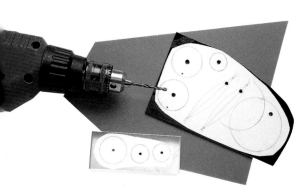

### Materials

- - - - - - - - - -

Black plexiglass sheet approx. 4 × 6¼ inches and ⅛ inch thick
·
Copper sheet approx. 1½ × 4 inches and 1/20 inch thick
·
Stick glue
·
Steel block
·
Steel punch
·
Small steel hammer with round-ball end
·
Power drill
·
Drill stand
·
Drill bits – ¼ inch, 7/64 inch, and 1/16 inch

Jeweler's saw with coarse and fine blades
·
Coarse and fine metal files
·
800 grit emery paper or finer
·
Ultrafine paint brush
·
Enamel paints in silver, black, brass, and bronze
·
Round copper tube 3/32-inch diameter
·
Steel point
·
Brooch pin
·
Epoxy glue
·
Ear wires

- - - - - - - - - -

**1** Trace the templates (above) on paper. Cut as follows: three of A, one of B, two of C, two of D, and one of E. Glue B and two of A onto the copper. Glue the remaining shapes onto the plexiglass. Place the copper on a steel block, put a steel punch where the holes are to be drilled, and tap with a steel hammer. Drill using a power drill mounted vertically on a stand. On the plexiglass, drill the six large holes using a 7/64-inch drill bit. With a ¼-inch drill bit, countersink the holes on *one* side of each perspex shape. Use this drill bit to remove the burr around the holes in the copper. With a 1/16-inch drill bit, drill a hole close to the edge of each circle.

### Templates

Copper
Ⓐ two ¾in circles
Ⓑ one 1⅛in circle

Plexiglass
Ⓐ one ¾in circle
Ⓒ two 1⅜in circles
Ⓓ one moon shape, cut from a 2⅜in circle
Ⓔ two canoe shapes, 2¾in long

**2** With a jeweler's saw, cut out the shapes as close to the outside of the outlines as possible. Use a coarse blade to cut the plexiglass and a fine blade for the copper. Don't worry if the saw lines aren't perfect.

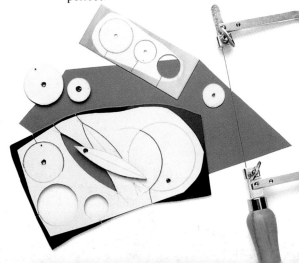

**3** File all the edges down to the outlines, using a coarse file for the plexiglass and a fine file for the copper. Make sure all the saw marks are cleaned off, and remove the burr created by cutting gently with the file. Remove the paper and soak the pieces in hot water to remove all traces of glue. Lay the 800-grit emery paper on a hard, flat surface and rub the surfaces of the plexiglass over it for an even finish.

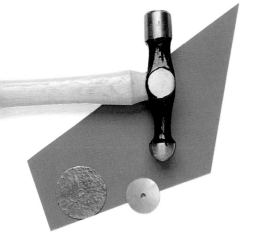

**4** Put each copper shape on the steel block and, using the round ball end of a small steel hammer, lightly hammer the entire surface to give an even texture.

**5** Before painting the plexiglass, check you are painting the correct sides. On pieces A and D, paint the side where the hole is countersunk. On the other three pieces, paint the opposite side. This is very important, as the countersinking provides a space for the rivets. Using an ultrafine paintbrush and enamels, decorate the shapes as shown. Wait for each color to dry thoroughly before applying the next. Place the pieces on a baking sheet and put them in the oven or under the broiler on the lowest setting for 3–5 minutes to harden the paint. Make sure the paint does not bubble and the plexiglass does not start to curl up at the edges.

**6** File the end of the copper tube flat with a fine file. Place the pieces in order on the steel block. Put the tube in the hole of one earring. With a steel point, mark the tube $\frac{1}{12}$ inch above the top of the earring, then cut off with a jeweler's saw. File the cut end flat. Repeat for all the pieces. Stand the pieces of tube in each hole, place a steel punch over each one, and tap lightly on both sides with a steel hammer. Repeat for all the pieces. Attach findings to the brooch and earrings.

# *Marbled bead necklace*

Creating your own marbled beads is a simple process with today's synthetic modeling clays. There is a dazzling palette of colors available which can produce spectacular results when mixed together.

**1** Break off a small piece of Fimo from one block and knead with your fingers until soft and pliable. Roll it out on a flat surface to form a thin sausage shape, using the palms of your hands. Repeat with the other remaining blocks. Braid the different colors together, then twist and start to knead the colors together.

## Materials

• • •

3 blocks of Fimo or other polymer clay, in contrasting colors

Craft knife

Wooden skewers

Block of modeling clay

Varnish

Strong thread (colored raffia is ideal)

Superglue

• • •

*Colors blend when Fimo is twisted*

**2** Roll the kneaded Fimo into a sausage shape, fold in half, twist the two halves together and knead again. Continue twisting and kneading until all the air bubbles have gone and you achieve a marbled effect.

**3** Roll the clay into a sausage shape again. Cut off small pieces with a craft knife and roll them into balls between the palms of your hands. Make as many balls as you need for the length of necklace required, rolling out more pieces of Fimo if necessary.

**4** Push a wooden skewer through each ball to make a central hole, then gently remove the "bead" and insert the skewer from the other end. Smooth any rough edges by gently rolling the bead between the palms of your hands again. Thread the beads carefully back onto the skewers and fire in a low oven, following the manufacturer's instructions. Leave to cool.

**6** Thread the beads onto raffia or other strong thread to the length required. Tie a double knot and fix with a dab of glue. Push the ends back through the beads to conceal them.

Varnish beads on wooden skewers

**5** Spray or paint with varnish to bring out the true depth of the colors, then leave to dry.

## ⋅⋅⋅ INSPIRATIONS

**Dazzling and dramatic results are easily achieved using modern plastics and synthetic clays to make jewelry.**

**1** Beads and synthetic clay in rich baroque colors create a stunning pendant and earrings. *Kate Smith*

**2** Bold geometric patterns are hand-painted on these clay earrings. *Pat Thomas*

**3** Acrylic jewelry in strong shapes with bright fish motifs. *Rowena Park*

**4** Clay brooches in abstract shapes are part-glazed to emphasize the decoration. *Paolo Iori*

**5** Fimo is mixed and marbled then cut to shape to form the basis of these contemporary earrings. *Penny and Jessica Burdett*

**6 & 7** Acrylic bangle and brooch in vibrant colors and sharp modern designs. *Stephanie Burke*

**8** Pretty clay brooch in pastel colors highlighted with black. *The Hands Work*

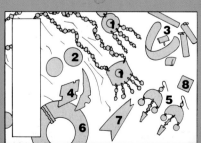

# TREASURES FOR FREE

# 5
...

# TREaSURES
# FoR FRee
.....

# Treasures for free

■ ■ ■ **What can be more rewarding than making something beautiful out of trash or something you've just happened upon? It's an extremely cheap and environmentally friendly hobby, and once you start, you'll be amazed at what can spark off an idea. With basic jewelry skills, you can create stylish pieces from almost anything you can find.**

Household trash can be a great source of un-usual materials – soft-drink cans, for example, make witty earrings. The new-style cans don't have dangerously sharp edges and are easy to cut into simple shapes with a cutting tool known as tin snips, available from hardware stores. Be inspired by bits and pieces found in your tool box, and create neck-laces and earrings from metal washers and nuts and bolts. If they look a little rusty, you can simply sand them and give them a new lease of life with a coat of bright paint.

Absolutely anything can be used to make an unusual decoration. One talented young designer incorporated pieces from a broken car blinker light into her designs; another embellished a teaspoon with clasps from broken necklaces and bracelets to create a stunning, baroque-style brooch.

Tailgate and yard sales are paradise for the jeweler who plans to create masterpieces from junk. They are perfect places for picking up broken necklaces or watches, flatware, bits of wire, and old buttons. The seashore is another great provider of materials and ideas – shells can be strung into necklaces, driftwood can be varnished and made into splendid earrings, pebbles can be wrapped decoratively with silver wire and transformed into pendants.

The possibilities are endless. Once hooked, you will find yourself becoming a scavenger, looking at absolutely anything and wondering if it could be transformed into earrings or a brooch.  ■ ■ ■

# China and bamboo necklace

Don't despair if one of your prized china plates gets broken – turn it into a necklace!

Or, use our project as a guide and wrap a pretty seashell or pebble with wire, or any other unusual object you might find.

**1** Choose a piece of broken china as your centerpiece. Our piece measures about 1½ inches x 2½ inches. File the edges of the china until smooth, but make sure to keep it an interesting shape.

## Materials

• • •

Bamboo cane

Silver wire

Leather thong

Colored stain or felt-tip marking pens

Clear matte varnish

One piece of broken china

File or sandpaper

Wire cutters

Flat-nose pliers

Round-nose pliers

Small saw

Strong knitting needle or awl

• • •

**2** Cut an 18 inch length of wire, then file the ends. Make a u-shaped loop in the wire about 6¼ inches down; the actual position of the loop depends on the piece of china. Wrap the short end around the china and at right angles up through the U-loop.

**3** Next, wrap the long piece of wire around three times. Take the long length through the U-loop and bring it up over the top of the china, then down the front and wrap it around the bands of wire at the front. Coil the loose ends three times around the piece of wire that you just brought down the front.

**4** Bring the wire up to the top of the china and form a loop about ½ inch taller than the china shape. Wrap the other piece of wire tightly around the bottom of the loop. The wire should be tight enough to hold the china securely.

**5** To make the wire coils, cut a 7 inch length of wire and neatly curl in one end with the round-nose pliers. Begin coiling the wire around itself, holding it steady with the flat-nose pliers. Make a loop out of the last ¾ inch, then turn the loop at right angles to the coil so that it will lie flat on the necklace.

with a knitting needle or awl. Use stain or marker pens to color the bamboo in a hue that complements the china. Coat with matte varnish to seal and leave to dry.

**6** To make the wire springs, wrap a length of wire around a pencil five times. Bend in any ends that stick out. Repeat for a total of 8 springs. Make eight large springs by wrapping longer lengths of wire 8 times around the pencil.

**8** Thread the china onto a leather thong. Add one small spring and one ringed bamboo section on either side. Next, add a short spring, a coil and short spring on both sides, followed by plain bamboo. Continue working both sides, alternating ringed and plain bamboo pieces with large springs between. Finish on both sides with a short spring.

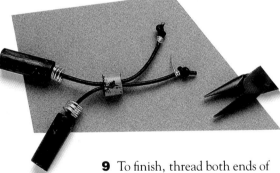

**9** To finish, thread both ends of the leather through the small piece of bamboo. Knot the ends of the leather and trim if necessary. Cut a small piece of wire and, using the flat-nosed pliers, wrap it around the ends of the leather just above the knot.

**7** With the saw, cut six 1½ inch lengths of bamboo, choosing sections that have rings. Cut six more smooth bamboo sections about 1 inch long, then cut one ½ inch piece. File the ends smooth, then make a hole down the middle of each

These wonderful old coins were spotted in a seondhand store and snapped up by the designer, who thought they would make unusual

# *Shipwreck coin jewelry*

but elegant jewelry. They look especially good with a gold-plated finish – a reputable jeweler should be able to arrange for your coins to be dipped, a process that is not as expensive as it sounds. If you don't want to go to this trouble, a similar effect can be achieved with good-quality gold paint and varnish.

**1** Make small holes on opposite sides of each coin, using a drill with a fine bit that is suitable for metal.

## Materials
• • •
Selection of old coins
•
Drill
•
Pliers
•
Wire cutters (if not part of pliers)
•
Gold or silver wire
•
Length of chain with large links
•
Jump ring
•
Bolt ring
•
Ear wires
•
Gold paint, paint brush, and varnish (optional)
• • •

**3** Using the same technique, thread the opposite end of the wire through another coin. Continue linking the coins until you have the length required.

**2** Use wire cutters to trim the wire into 1½-inch lengths. Thread a piece of wire through a hole in one coin, winding it back over itself to secure. Make sure the loop is large enough to allow the coin to hang freely.

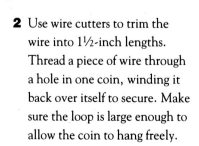

**4** Attach a piece of chain about 1 inch long to one end by threading the wire from the last coin through the end link of the chain, using the same technique as before to secure it. Fix a jump ring to the last link of the chain at the opposite end.

**5** Take a piece of chain long enough to form a necklace the required length and fasten it to the other end of the coins in the same way as above. Complete by securing a bolt ring to the last link.

**6** To make the earrings, simply drill a single hole in each coin. Using pliers, open the loop at the bottom of an ear wire, push this through the hole, and secure. Have the coins gold-plated, or paint them yourself with gold paint, then spray or paint on varnish.

# Tin Can Earrings

These imaginative earrings are made by recycling tin cans, so they are perfect for these environmentally aware times. The designs can be as witty or as sophisticated as you like.

**Important** Take care when working with metal. Protect your eyes and hands while cutting and file all edges smooth to avoid accidents.

## Tin Spirals

*You don't need any expensive equipment to create these impressive earrings. The can is easily cut and shaped using a craft knife and tin snips.*

### Materials
• • •
1 soft drink can
·
Tin snips
·
Craft knife
·
Metal ruler
·
Pencil
·
Hammer
·
Small nail
·
Ear wires
·
Pliers
·
Selection of tiny glass or plastic jewel stones
·
Craft glue suitable for metal
• • •

**1** Remove the top of the can using tin snips, then wash the can in soapy water and leave to dry. Cut down the side of the can and remove the base. Lay the can out flat on a board and score three parallel lines along its length with a craft knife and metal ruler. The metal should be pliable enough for you to separate the strips by bending along the lines.

**2** Wrap each strip around a pencil to form a spiral; hold in place for a couple of minutes. Slip the metal off the pencil and trim to the required length.

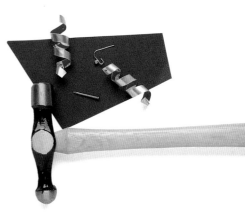

**3** Use a hammer and small nail to pierce a hole at the top of each spiral, then attach an ear wire with pliers.

**4** Decorate each spiral by gluing tiny jewel stones all over.

## Crystal Drops

*Nobody would ever guess that these dazzling drop earrings are created out of an old can. Crystal beads add extra sparkle.*

### Materials
• • •
1 small can
•
Can opener
•
Tin snips
•
Hammer
•
Metal ruler
•
Pencil
•
Craft knife
•
Metal file
•
Pliers
•
Small nail
•
2 crystal drop beads
•
Jump rings
•
Ear wires
• • •

**1** Soak the can in warm, soapy water to remove the label, then rinse thoroughly to remove all traces of its contents. Leave to dry. Remove the base using a can opener, then cut down one side with tin snips. Lay the metal on a board and gently hammer the seamed outer edges to make it lie flat. (The outside of the can, i.e. the shiny side, will be the right side.)

**2** Using a metal ruler, mark two squares in pencil on the can and score along the pencil lines with a craft knife. Cut out the shapes with tin snips, then file all the edges smooth. Using pliers, turn the tip of each corner to the wrong side to blunt them.

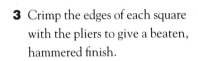

**3** Crimp the edges of each square with the pliers to give a beaten, hammered finish.

**4** Use a hammer and small nail to make a hole at the top of each shape for an ear wire, then one at the bottom for a drop bead. Secure the ear wires and beads with jump rings.

# *Bold beads and beasts*

This splendid necklace has been made using an eclectic mix of beads picked up cheaply at yard sales.

## Materials

Mixed beads in different sizes
·
Strong nylon thread
·
Needle
·
Jewelry wire
·
Clasp and calotte crimp beads from a broken necklace
·
Pliers
·
Modeling clay
·
Wallpaper paste
·
Newspaper
·
Craft knife
·
White glue
·
Paints
·
Paint brushes
·
Varnish
·
Eye pins
· · ·

**1** Make a large knot at one end of a thread that is the required length for your necklace. Thread on the beads, mixing them together to create an interesting effect.

Squeeze a calotte crimp bead tightly over the knots at each end of the necklace. Attach the necklace clasp using pliers, one section to the loops on each calotte crimp bead (a bolt ring and split ring have been used here).

**2** To make the beaded hoops, cut pieces of jewelry wire to the length required, allowing a little extra for securing and joining to the necklace. Bend one end of each length with pliers, to stop the beads from falling straight off, then thread on as required. Bend the other end of the wire, then twist the ends together. Join to the necklace by twisting the wire over the thread between two beads.

**3** Next, cut several different lengths of wire to make bead drops. Loop one end of each piece of wire with pliers, thread on as many beads as required, then use the pliers to form a hook at the opposite end. Attach to the necklace as before.

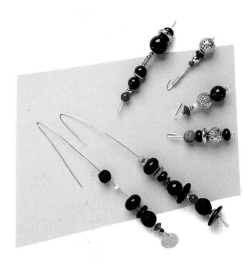

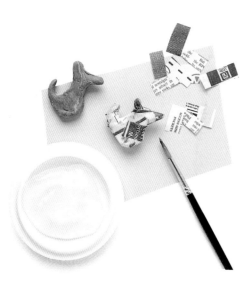

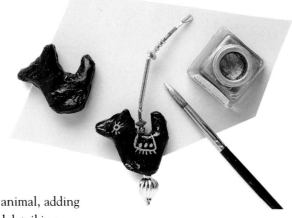

**4** Make a mold in the required shape from modeling clay. Mix the wallpaper paste using hot water, then tear the newspaper into small, neat pieces. Paste the clay mold with several layers of newspaper until completely covered and firm. Leave to dry.

**6** Paint each animal, adding features and detail in a contrasting color, then finish with one or two coats of varnish. When completely dry, carefully pierce the papier-mâché animals with a needle from bottom to top. Thread a couple of beads onto an eye pin, then push the pin through the papier-mâché and out the other side. Add a few more beads, then make a loop at the end of the pin. Thread small beads onto two more eye pins, join all three together to form a long drop, and secure to the necklace by looping the end of the last pin over the nylon thread between two beads.

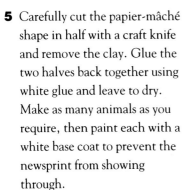

**5** Carefully cut the papier-mâché shape in half with a craft knife and remove the clay. Glue the two halves back together using white glue and leave to dry. Make as many animals as you require, then paint each with a white base coat to prevent the newsprint from showing through.

# Twisted wire bangles

It is amazing what can be created from things found lying around in the garage. The designer made these unusual bangles by cleverly twisting different-colored wires together using a simple hand drill and was then inspired to try braiding and hammering to gain even more attractive results.

## Materials

• • •

2 yards each of nickel and copper wire 0.75 mm (1⁄30 inch) thick

•

Wire cutters

•

Hand drill

•

Vice (optional)

•

Pliers

•

Small can

•

Mallet (optional)

• • •

**1** Cut each length of wire in half and bunch the pieces together. Clamp one end into a hand drill and the other into a vice or a tight drawer to hold them firm, making sure that all the wires are held in the same place so they are an even length. Pull the wires taut.

**Important** Take care when working with metal wire as it can break, causing the ends to fly around at great speed. Protect your eyes and hands, and blunt all ends.

**2** Without allowing the wires to slacken, slowly turn the handle of the drill. The wires will start to twist around each other as shown, but if you allow the tension to slacken, they will just become tangled. Continue winding until the twist is as tight as you want it, and is even along the whole length. Pull the wires sharply to set the twist, then remove from the drill and vice (or drawer).

**3** Using pliers, curl the ends of each wire into a loop so that they won't scratch when worn.

**5** You can use twisted wire to make a variety of designs. Try flattening the wire with a hammer, making a plaited version, or using different types and thicknesses of wire.

**4** Wrap the twisted wire around a small can several times, keeping the loops at each end facing out. Choose a can that is a little wider than the part of your arm you wish to wear the bangle on. Push the wire against the can to shape it, or use a mallet if the coil of wire is too stiff. Carefully remove the finished bangle from the can.

Turning junk into wearable jewelry can be an addictive hobby, often producing

# *Chrome and crystal jewelry*

outrageous results. The bits and pieces found in the bottom of a workshop tool box provided the inspiration for these unusual, yet stylish earrings, with a heart-shaped crystal bead adding the perfect finishing touch. The same basic materials and techniques can be used to make a coordinating bracelet to complete the look.

## Materials

• • •

Epoxy glue

2 metal wheel hub caps

Ear clips with integral loops

Jump rings

2 medium metal washers

Small metal washers (10 for earrings plus plenty more for bracelet)

Pliers

2 small split rings

2 short lengths of chain

3 crystal beads

2 small nuts

Head pin

Wire cutters

Bolt ring clasp

• • •

Ear clip

Hub cap

**2** For each earring: using jump rings throughout, first join a medium washer to a small washer. Next, join four small washers in pairs, as shown, to the initial small washer, securing the jump rings with pliers. Add a dab of glue to the point where both ends of the jump ring meet.

**1** Using a strong epoxy, glue each hub cap to an ear clip and leave to dry for 24 hours.

Crystal bead

First small washer

Nut

Split ring

Head pin

Crystal bead

Jump ring

Ear clip

Medium washer

**3** Slip a split ring through one end of a length of chain and a jump ring through the other. Use the jump ring to join the chain to the first small washer, centrally between the other two, as illustrated. Using jump rings again, join a crystal bead and a nut to the washers.

**4** To complete the earrings, use a jump ring to join the medium washer to the ear clip, pushing it through the loop.

**5** To make the matching bracelet, simply join small washers together with jump rings until you have the correct length to fit your wrist comfortably. Thread the head pin through a crystal bead, trim the excess wire with cutters, and turn a loop. Insert a jump ring through the loop and join to the bracelet, linking jump ring to jump ring as shown. Open up the loop on the clasp with pliers and attach it to the final jump ring. Repeat for the other side.

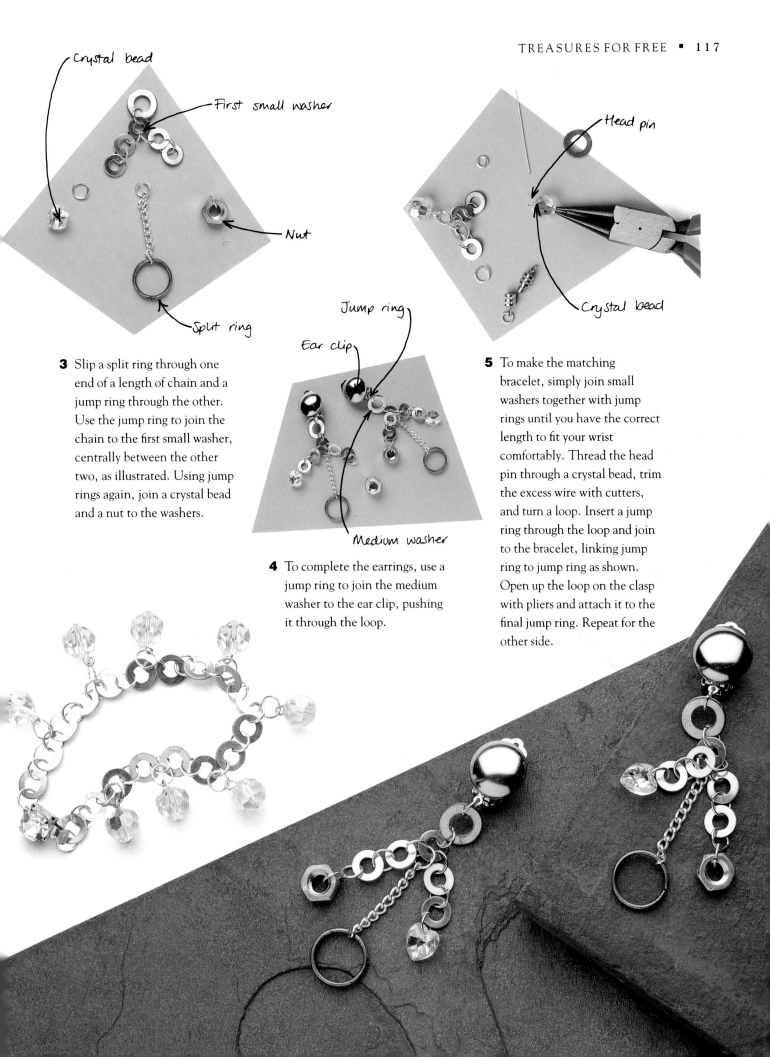

Broken watches can be given a new lease of life with just a little imagination. These

# Time pieces

witty earrings and barette have been put together using the decorative faces and mechanisms of both pocket and wrist-watches, collected from yard sales for very little cost.

**1** Carefully open up each watch with a screwdriver and separate the parts. Clean gently but thoroughly with a soft cloth.

**3** Make three bead drops for each earring and fasten them to a watch mechanism by threading them through existing holes and knotting securely. Add a dab of glue to hold the knots firmly in place. Decorate the front of each mechanism with attractive cogs and small beads glued in place. To complete, glue an ear clip on the back of each earring.

### Materials

• • •

A selection of
broken watches
•
Screwdriver
•
Strong thread
•
Needle
•
Small gilt beads
•
Epoxy glue
•
Ear clips
•
Barette

• • •

**2** To make the earrings select a decorative watch cog, knot a length of strong thread to it, and string on several small gilt beads to form a drop.

**5** Build up your design on the barette by gluing the watch faces and several decorative cogs securely in place.

**4** To make the barette, select several watch faces and remove the hands from all except one. Glue the hands on this one to set them in position.

# Ostentatious ostrich brooch

Many people are daunted by the thought of working with metal because they assume that some technical skill or expensive equipment is involved. However, this is not necessarily the case. The sheet tin used here can be cut and shaped like any piece of fabric, using inexpensive tin snips. The finished piece is then painted in bright enamel hobby paints. You can buy sheet tin from hardware stores, but a cheaper alternative is to use an old tin can. Any large, heavy, square-shaped can, such as an olive oil can, is suitable.

*Template*

## Materials

• • •

Piece of sheet tin
about 4 × 6 inches
•
Tracing paper
•
Pen or pencil
•
Tin snips
•
Rubber-headed or
hide hammer
•
Small metal file
•
Mineral spirits
•
Enamel hobby
paints in a variety
of colors
•
Paint brushes
•
Epoxy glue
•
Brooch pin
•
Varnish

• • •

**1** Trace the brooch from the template, cut it out, and transfer the outline to the tin.

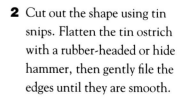

**2** Cut out the shape using tin snips. Flatten the tin ostrich with a rubber-headed or hide hammer, then gently file the edges until they are smooth.

**3** Wipe the surface of the brooch with a cloth dipped in mineral spirits to remove any grease, then paint in the base colors with enamel paints. Allow the paint to dry thoroughly.

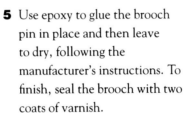

**5** Use epoxy to glue the brooch pin in place and then leave to dry, following the manufacturer's instructions. To finish, seal the brooch with two coats of varnish.

**4** Using a small brush, add the decorative detail such as the spots, stripes, and features. Leave to dry overnight.

# INSPIRATIONS

**Innovative "found" jewelry is designed around the most unusual objects to create spectacular pieces.**

**1** Ornate jewelry made from found beads and broken mirror glass embedded in resin *Andrew Logan*

**2** Shells from the seashore and pieces of mirror glass are embedded in resin to make this brooch. *Andrew Logan*

**3** Handmade paper decorated with scraps of metal makes great earrings. *Deirdre Hawken*

**4** Stunning laurel crown made from fine copper leaves decorated with clock parts. *Deirdre Hawken*

**5** Genuine bone has been used to make this unusual decorative pin. *Deirdre Hawken*

**6** Rubber tubing and matting are transformed into a modern bangle. *Lyn Medcalf*

**7** An assortment of silver-colored found objects combine to make witty drop earrings. *Michael de Nardo*

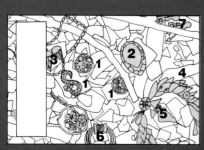

# Contributors

## CHAPTER 1

*Beaded brooch*
**JANET COLES BEADS**
Perdiswell Cottage
Bilford Road
Worcester

*Tiffany-style Necklace*
**LIZ GILL**
98 West End Lane
London NW6

*Art Deco Beadwork*
**ELISE MANN**
54 Tiverton Road
Edgware
Middlesex

*Thousand Flower Beads*
**DEBORAH ALEXANDER**
14 Barrington Road
Horsham
West Sussex

*Black and White Beads*
**KATE SMITH**
46 Crompton Street
Derby
Derbyshire

*Button Treasures*
**SAMMIE BELL**
25b Richmond Avenue
Islington
London N1

*Others*
**JO MOODY**
50 Kingwood Road
Fulham
London SW6

## CHAPTER 2

*Romantic Lace Rosettes*
**JO MOODY**
50 Kingwood Road
Fulham
London SW6

*High-Tech Brooch & Earrings*
**LYNN MEDCALF**
102 Railton Road
Brixton
London SE24

*Vivid Felt Brooch*
**JO MOODY**
50 Kingwood Road
Fulham
London SW6

*Vibrant Knitted Necklace*
**MANDY NASH**
Model House
Bullring
Llantrisant
Mid Glamorgan

*Sumptuous Silk*
**KAREN HOWSE**
2 St Thomas Hill
Launceston
Cornwall

*Richness From Rags*
**JUDY CLAYTON**
Flat 3
16 Chesham Place
Kemptown
Brighton
East Sussex

## CHAPTER 3

*Rolled Paper Beads*
**ELISE MANN**
54 Tiverton Road
Edgware
Middlesex

*Mediterranean Magic*
**JACKIE SCHOU**
7 Croft Gardens
Alton
Hampshire

*Dramatic Paper & Paste Earrings*
**JACKIE SCHOU**
7 Croft Gardens
Alton
Hampshire

*Papier maché Bracelet*
**KATE SMITH**
46 Crompton Street
Derby
Derbyshire

*Hand-crafted Paper Brooch*
**HAMMIE TAPPENDEN**
The Old Bakery
Locks Green
Porchfield
Isle of Wight

*Quilled Filigree*
**ELISE MANN**
54 Tiverton Road
Edgware
Middlesex

*Origami*
**ELISE MANN**
54 Tiverton Road
Edgware
Middlesex

# CHAPTER 4

*Valentine Hearts*
**JO MOODY**
50 Kingwood Road
Fulham
London SW6

*Contemporary Chic*
**KATE SMITH**
46 Crompton Street
Derby
Derbyshire

*Inca-inspired Necklace*
**LINDSEY STOCK**
127 Wakeman Road
Kensal Green
London NW10

*Seashell Hairslide & Earrings*
**ANGELA CAIRD**
10 Park Road
Aldershot
Hampshire

*Harlequin Hearts*
**ELISE MANN**
54 Tiverton Road
Edgware
Middlesex

*Zig-Zag Copper*
**STEPHANIE BURKE**
2 Brunswick Street
St Pauls
Bristol
Avon

*Marbled Beads*
**JO MOODY**
50 Kingwood Road
Fulham
London SW6

# CHAPTER 5

*China & Bamboo*
**SARA WITHERS**
Old Cottage
Appleton, Abingdon
Oxon

*Shipwreck Coins*
**THERIE SHEA**
20 The Woodlands
Esher
Surrey

*Tin Can Earrings*
**JO MOODY**
50 Kingwood Road
Fulham
London SW6

*Bold Beads & Beasts*
**JACKIE SCHOU**
7 Croft Gardens
Alton
Hampshire

*Twisted Wire Bangles*
**ELISE MANN**
54 Tiverton Road
Edgware
Middlesex

*Chrome & Crystal*
**JO MOODY**
50 Kingwood Road
Fulham
London SW6

*Time Pieces*
**SAMMIE BELL**
25b Richmond Avenue
Islington
London N1

*Ostentatious Ostrich*
**MARION ELLIOT**
Unit 7
Omnibus Workspace
39–41 North Road
London N7

. . . . . .

*Ceramic background*
**CHRISTINE CONSTANCE**

*Beads pages 18–19 and
40–41 supplied by*
**CREATIVE BEADCRAFT LTD**
**ELLS & FARRIER**
20 Beak Street
London W1

# Index